MW01292141

# Custo

## *and the*

# *Imitation*

## *of*

# *hrist*

A Spiritual Adventure in the Workplace

# *Ron Johnson*

RON JOHNSON

ISBN: 1468162055
ISBN-13:9781468162059

# DEDICATION

I am grateful to

Stacie Webster, Kimberly Wells, and Jane Lawson

for taking a chance on an out-of-work professor back in the fall of 2000. This book is dedicated to them and to my coworkers on the Resource Center from 2002 to 2005:

David Ascoli, Sam Flick, Tiffany King, Eileen Lawrence, Natalie Mallory, Kathleen Robins, Rudi Sanchez, Nancy Shue, and our supervisor, Deushawn Saunders.

When we were together, it almost didn't seem like work.

# CONTENTS

# ACKNOWLEDGMENTS

The cover was designed by Adam Goldberg.

Unless otherwise noted, the Scripture quotations contained herein are from the New Revised Standard Version Bible, copyright © 1989 by the Division of Christian Education of the National Council of the Churches of Christ in the U.S.A., and are used by permission. All rights reserved.

The quotation on page 75 is from E. Stanley Jones, *The Christ of the Mount: A Working Philosophy of Life* (NY: Abingdon Press, 1931), p. 85.

I want to thank my wife Nancy and daughter Emily for providing encouragement and helpful insights. I am also grateful to Senior Pastor Barry Petrucci and the members of Portage Chapel Hill United Methodist Church in Portage, Michigan (USA) for offering moral support.

# 1 BEATING THE CSR BLUES

Are you a customer service representative (CSR)? So am I. You know what they're saying about us? We're the bad guys. We're an example of what's wrong with the world today. They're saying that we don't care about our clients… that we just want to get them off the phone… that they have to call several times before anyone will help them.

You know what's sad? They're right.

I'm not saying we're bad people. I'm just saying there are a lot of CSRs who fit that description, and it's hard for the rest of us to turn things around. The role we play practically forces us to behave the way the public perceives us. We may have been nice before we took this position, but the job itself lays its own constraints on us.

I believe it's natural for most human beings to want to help others, but once we become CSRs, it's hard to do that consistently.

Let's begin with the positive side of this. If we're in our right minds, most of us want to be helpful. Imagine a mother with several small children stranded on the side of the highway. Black smoke is billowing out of her engine, and her kids are still strapped into their seats. Wouldn't you stop to help? You may not know anything about cars, but wouldn't you at least try to get her children to safety?

Or suppose you're in a restaurant and someone chokes on his meal. Nobody around him knows the Heimlich Maneuver. You just took a class in life-saving techniques two days ago. Would you turn to the person beside you and say, "Please pass the steak sauce"?

We've all heard of cases in which someone died shouting for help and nobody lifted a finger, but those are usually situations involving violence. The bystanders either don't know what to do or are too scared—or too scarred—to pitch in. Under normal circumstances, people sympathize with others in need and offer their assistance eagerly.

In other words, what we CSRs do for a living is a natural thing for human beings to do. Most people want to help others. We ourselves do when we're not at our place of employment. But there are a number of features of customer service work that make it hard for us to do that when we're answering the phones.

### Why It's Hard for CSRs to Give Good Service

First, there are so many customers and they come at us so fast that they all blur together in our minds. Some CSRs have contact with hundreds of customers each day. "I spoke with you earlier this week," a client says. "Don't you remember me?" Many of our customers ask the same questions or have the same complaints. We find ourselves repeating stock phrases. Sometimes we hear ourselves talking but our minds are wandering.

Second, many of the people we serve are angry, and they take their anger out on us. Maybe if we had heard about their problem second- or third-hand, we would have been sympathetic. But many customers turn us off immediately by treating us unkindly. They're frustrated, and they want to take their frustration out on somebody. It's natural for them to take it out on us, but it's also natural for us to get defensive or to tell them, "That's not my area. You need to talk to Department X."

Third, we're expected to project a sense of enthusiasm and sympathy even when we don't feel enthusiastic or sympathetic. It's not just putting aside our personal problems and focusing on the customer. Any professional has to do that. But CSRs have to appear cheerful and deeply interested in whatever the customer is saying. "I hate having to be 'on' all the time," one of my coworkers once said.

To complicate matters, there are many times in which we truly *aren't* interested in the customers' complaints. Perhaps we think they're being petty or demanding. This means we often have to pretend that we care. I once heard about a firm that specializes in training customer service personnel to do precisely that. "The key to good customer service is not to care about the customer," they say. "It's to *act* like you care." So they offer acting lessons! We may smile, but you and I know that there's a particle of truth to that.

Fourth, all of this takes place under the watchful eyes of quality control managers. It's their job to critique us. "You forgot to tell the customer to have a nice day," they say, or: "You missed a perfect opportunity to remind them about our online services." The problem is, there's always something more we could've said or done. The quality control people are there to point out to us the things that didn't come naturally at the time—the things we might have said or done in a perfect world. Unfortunately, it's not a perfect world.

To reinforce the quality mindset, they often give us cute phrases or tag lines that we have to include in our conversations. "Thank you for choosing Bud's Market. May I interest you in our fine assortment of Peter Piper's Handpicked Peck of Pickled Peppers?"

Or, "Welcome to the People's Favorite Bank, Home of Hassle-Free Checking. Would you like to open a Hassle-Free Checking account today? I promise not to hassle you if you open one. Here's a pen."

In either case, if we do the natural thing—that is, if just we smile and say hello—we'll get a poor evaluation. If we get poor evaluations then we won't get bonuses or promotions, and if it happens enough times we may even be fired. So we have to do the unnatural thing in order to excel in our job.

Fifth, we also have managers telling us to work faster. In call centers there are mounds of statistics showing the average length of our calls, our average wrap-up time after each call, the number of calls we take per day, and so on. And we're constantly pressured to improve these scores—to shorten the length of time we spend on each client.

On one side, then, we have the quality control people marking us down for neglecting anything we *might* have said, and on the other side we have managers urging us to serve each client faster. Sometimes we get both messages from the same manager.

Put it all together and it's easy to see why our natural inclination to help others doesn't carry over into our job. We talk to other human beings all day and yet we're expected to relate to them in unnatural ways: to repeat canned phrases, to use the customer's name at least twice during each conversation, to "put a smile in our voice," and a host of other things that interfere with our natural desire to help others. And our customers can tell.

Sixth—and perhaps most importantly—there are a lot of people in this business who don't want to be here. Many CSRs are college students studying to enter a different career after graduation. Others have been in customer service for years because it's the only work they can find. It's rare to meet frontline CSRs who love what they do. For the average Joe Shmoe, it's just a job.

Granted, this is not the only field that suffers from this problem. Lots of people devote their time and energy to work that means nothing to them. That's not something peculiar to us CSRs.

But customer service work brings us in direct contact with people who need us to care. So we either have to *learn* to care or else we have to put on a good show. Of course, there's a third alternative: to give poor service. And judging from statistics, that's the option of choice for many CSRs.

Managers do what they can. They pay outside companies a lot of money to survey us in hopes of discovering ways to motivate us. Then they meet with us to discuss the survey findings and they chart out action plans that are supposed to increase our job satisfaction. But if we CSRs aren't internally-motivated, then nothing management does will change how we feel. Although it may sound like I'm being a defeatist, it's true. If you're a CSR and you view customer service as just a job, then there's nothing management can do to make you feel differently. But I can tell you from experience that there *is* something *God* can do.

### *Opportunity Knocks*

I have a PhD in Philosophy. I love teaching, and for a few years after I earned my doctorate I was lucky enough to be in the classroom full-time. But I couldn't get a tenure track position. Competition was fierce, and I wasn't part of a brand-name graduate program. I'm proud to say that I got my degree from Saint Louis University, a fine Jesuit school. But name recognition is everything in the academic world, and I was competing against applicants from Princeton and Harvard. (It didn't help that I was a maverick and that my philosophical project was highly unusual.

But we won't go into that right now.) To support my family, I went back to the field I had been in before graduate school: I began working in a customer service call center by day and I taught college courses at night.

It wasn't what I wanted. But I was a disciple of Jesus Christ, and as I sought divine direction, I began to understand some things.

First, I realized that I was back in customer service for reasons beyond my control, and I believed that something as important as that doesn't happen by accident. Somehow in the scheme of things, it mattered that I was here doing this. I therefore accepted it as part of my calling, at least for the present. I hoped to return to full-time teaching later, but for right now I was determined to learn what I was called to do in this place and to do it.

Second, I began to see that customer service was an ideal venue for practicing my faith. Perhaps you've heard of the great Christian classic by Thomas à Kempis, *The Imitation of Christ*. Maybe you've even read it. But have you ever noticed that our line of work provides unique opportunities for *practicing* it? No other profession offers quite so many situations in which we must turn the other cheek or go the second mile. Few other jobs provide so many chances to help people in concrete ways or to move mountains on a daily basis. And if this job is temporary and we do something else for a living later on, no other profession will better prepare us to go forth and serve.

I accepted the challenge and it made all the difference. I

discovered that the life of a CSR can be more than just a job: it can be a holy calling. I soon demonstrated that I was good at soothing angry customers and especially at solving their problems. I made friends easily with people in other departments and, relying on that network of relationships, I was able to get things done for my clients. Before I had completed my first twelve months, my department named me "CSR of the Year." I was chosen to mentor new employees and was put on a committee dedicated to improving CSR quality.

I had stumbled back into the CSR role at the lowest point of my life, but it turned out to be exactly what I needed. I was discovering a new kind of spirituality: I was practicing the imitation of Christ *by means of customer service!* It saved me from a life of despair and, somewhat to my surprise, turned me into an effective CSR.

This book contains the meditations that have helped me to beat the CSR blues. No, this wasn't a career choice for me, but I have been cheered by a shimmering vision of what Christ wants me to do in my workplace. As I have tried to imitate him under these conditions, I have found a certain measure of peace—and sometimes even exhilaration—in being a CSR. In the pages ahead, I hope to communicate that vision to you.

### *Questions for Reflection and Discussion*

1.  Have you experienced any of the frustrating aspects of customer service work described in this chapter? Are there

others that weren't mentioned?

2. As a customer, have you yourself experienced poor customer service? As a CSR, can you understand what went wrong? If you were the CSR in that situation, how would you have handled it differently?

3. What qualities do you think a good CSR should have?

4. Suppose that managers all over the world made their CSRs take acting lessons, and we all became really good at *pretending* that we cared. Now imagine that CSRs all over the world were to begin imitating Christ and caring deeply about their customers. Which scenario would increase the level of service worldwide? Which one would improve the quality of life for CSRs?

# 2 SERVICE WITH A SMILE

It's the start of our shift. Marie, a friend of ours, comes into the office with her shoulders drooping, shuffling her feet. She plops down her purse and sighs heavily. "Oh, God," she moans. "Get me through another day."

People around her chuckle. This is Marie's morning mantra. We laugh, but it's also rather sad. Marie is a Christian. She keeps a Bible at her position and quotes from it frequently, but she lives like a victim, not a victor. To talk with her, you wouldn't know that she has direct access to the King of Kings.

Nor are we in a position to criticize her. As Christians, we should stand with shoulders back, head high in the air. Each day should be an adventure. And yet we, too, often feel that it's a struggle just to get through the workday. We're followers of the risen Christ. Can't we do better than that?

A study of the life of Christ suggests that we can. He shows us what it means to live powerful lives that are focused on others, not on ourselves. From him we can learn to face each new day with a sense of expectation.

Our first order of business is to want to serve our customers. This is where the imitation of Christ begins. In this regard, I have been especially inspired by the stories told in Matthew 8:1-4, 14-17. (The same stories are repeated, with some variation in the details, in Mark 1:32-42; Luke 5:12-16; and Luke 4:38-44.) These stories show Jesus on the lookout for people to whom he can minister. He seems genuinely enthusiastic about serving.

### *Not So Close*

We can hear it in his voice as he replies to a man stricken with leprosy. We have to put ourselves in Jesus' place to appreciate this. Imagine someone coming toward us whose skin has a vile disease, and it's highly contagious.

How do you think you would react? The natural thing would be to back away quickly. Most of us would probably do it without even thinking.

But if we were living in New Testament times, there's another reason why we would recoil at the sight of this man. Not only does he have a contagious disease, but our own scriptures condemn him for approaching us. Leviticus 13:45-46 requires those with leprosy to live outside the city, either alone or with other lepers. On their way out of town, they must warn those around them by shouting, "Unclean! Unclean!" This isn't just for sanitary reasons; a leper is considered unclean spiritually as well as physically. Whoever comes in contact with a leper—even unknowingly—also becomes unclean before God: "guilty," the law of Moses says (Leviticus 5:2-3).

We might shrug and say, "Yes, but Christ is going to heal him." But in the Old Testament, the prophet Elisha wouldn't even come out of his house to heal the leper Naaman (II Kings 5). Naaman was a high-ranking Syrian dignitary who was carrying a letter of introduction from his king. But Elisha wouldn't budge, even though Naaman was insulted by his refusal to talk to him face-to-face. Elisha sent out a messenger to tell Naaman what he had to do to be healed. Naaman was outraged. "Why doesn't he come out and wave his hands over me!" Naaman demanded. But Elisha wouldn't do it.

Of course, Elisha was probably trying to humble Naaman, who had arrived with his entourage expecting VIP treatment. But the law of Moses does say quite clearly that the Israelites are not to have any close contact with unclean people. And lepers are definitely unclean people, especially foreign lepers. Naaman was healed, but he didn't encounter the prophet in person; not until after he had been healed.

Here, then, is this vile leper coming right up to Jesus. He falls down at Christ's feet, and the damage is done. The Law of Moses says that he has defiled Jesus just by coming close to him. Again, if we were in Christ's place, both our natural inclinations and our religious upbringing would compel us to flee from the man, shouting imprecations at him over our shoulders.

12

But Jesus steps *toward* him.

The leper falls on his face before Jesus and cries, "If you want to, you can make me clean."

Jesus replies, "*I want to!*"

Then he reaches out and touches him. This is totally unnecessary. Christ often heals people without making physical contact. Sometimes he heals people who are on the other side of town (Luke 7:1-10; Mark 7:24-30). He doesn't have to touch the leper. He does it because he wants to.

"Be made clean!" he commands. And the man is healed.

"*I want to!*" Now *that* would make a great CSR mantra: "I *want* to help. I *want* to serve." Some of us might have grumbled, "Oh, all right. Be made clean, then." Or we might have been tempted to say, "You know, technically I shouldn't be doing this, but as a one-time courtesy. . ."

No. He says, "I want to!" Mark's gospel adds that he is "moved with compassion" (Mark 1:41, KJV). And it shows.

Notice that, when it's all over, the man doesn't even do what Jesus asks him to do. According to Leviticus 13, he's supposed to present himself to a priest for a physical inspection. He mustn't stop to see anyone else on the way. He must have a priest declare him clean and attest that he's eligible to live in town again. After that, he can do whatever he wants.

Biblical scholars also believe that Christ wants the man to help him keep the so-called "Messianic Secret." In other words, he doesn't want word to get out just yet that he's the Messiah. So, for both of these reasons, he charges the man not to tell anyone what has just happened to him. He must go and show himself to a priest. The man disobeys him. He's so excited, he runs around town telling everyone that Jesus has healed him. As a result, according to Mark's version of the story, the town gets worked up into such a frenzy that Jesus has to leave (Mark 1:45). But such disregard for his wishes doesn't douse Christ's enthusiasm. He doesn't walk away muttering, "That's the last time I'll stick my neck out for anybody." He continues to reach out to those in need.

### *A Long Night and an Early Morning*

It ends up being quite a day. He heals a centurion's servant and Peter's mother-in-law, but there are also many others to whom he ministers, long into the night. The entire town comes to his door. Sick and needy people visit him all evening, and he heals every one of them (Luke 4:40). Referring to a prophecy from Isaiah 53:4, Matthew describes him as taking people's infirmities upon himself (Matthew 8:17). He gets deeply and personally involved.

It's a long day. But we don't see him shooing people away or complaining about the lateness of the hour. He takes time to help and heal people.

The next morning, long before daybreak, he rises and finds a solitary place in which to pray (Mark 1:35). We aren't told what he's praying about, but we can guess, based on his remarks afterwards. He's praying about others, and about what he can do for them. He emerges from the session decisive and enthusiastic

14

about the course his ministry must take. His disciples find him and tell him everyone in town is looking for him, but he replies that it's time to move on to other cities. There are people in those places who need his ministry, too.

Taken all together, these episodes show Christ focusing on other people and enthusiastic about ministering to them. He doesn't just help them; he *wants* to help them. He works late into the night, then gets up early the next morning to meet with his Father to consider ways to help people better.

## *What It's Like to be a Customer*

Even though you and I do customer service for a living, we're also customers ourselves. And we know how hard it is to get good help.

Suppose we have a complaint about a product or service. We call the company's 800 number and the person who answers the call couldn't care less. He just tries to get us off the phone as quickly as he can.

We call back and a lady comes on the line with a confrontational attitude. She seems to be on a tight schedule and doesn't have time to listen to us. Without even asking about the details of our problem, she rattles off something about company policy. We keep trying to interrupt but she doesn't give us a chance. The next thing we know, we're listening to a dial tone.

Now we're mad. We call back and demand to speak to someone who can help us. We get passed around from one extension to another. "That's not my department," several people tell us, but none of them can identify the person to whom we should be talking. We're thinking about hiring a lawyer and taking it all the way to the Supreme Court if necessary.

And then. . .

We hear a friendly voice. She introduces herself and asks detailed questions about our problem. She doesn't hurry us. She seems truly sorry about the trouble we're having, and she regrets that we've been transferred so many times. Best of all, she takes personal responsibility for helping us resolve our problem. She gives us her full name and phone number and invites us to call her back any time we wish, but she promises to call us back with an update by 5 P.M. today.

When we hang up the phone, we're encouraged. Unfortunately, it's not unusual to be faced with apathy and even antagonism from the very people who are supposed to be serving us. But this woman's attitude is unusual. She sounds like she will help us, but more importantly, she sounds like she *wants* to do so. That's rare.

### *Do You Want To?*

Now let's put our customer service hats back on. We should ask ourselves the following question, being as honest as possible:

*If a customer in the situation I just described were to be transferred to us, what would they say about us afterwards?*

*Would they compare us to the apathetic representative who first answered the phone? Would they say that we were like the confrontational rep? Would they group us with the long list of people who said they couldn't do anything? Or would they say that we were like the last person—the one who genuinely wanted to help?*

For most of us, it probably depends on the day. Sometimes we live up to our highest ideals, while other times we fall short. But the question you and I need to think about is simply this: Do we *want* to help? Circumstances may prevent us from being helpful in every customer interaction. But *wanting* to help is the key. If we want to, then we can work on overcoming the obstacles to doing so. Lack of desire is the biggest hurdle.

I once told a friend and coworker about my vision of customer service as the imitation of Christ. "Ugh!" she replied. "I already know how to be servile. Why would I want to make a practice of it?" But we're not talking about being servile. We're talking about becoming like Jesus. Although he was always serving, he was never servile. I think about him smiling, stepping forward eagerly, and saying to unlovely people, "I want to help!" And that makes me want to do the same. He isn't here right now—not physically, anyway—but I am. And if I can do anything at this moment to share his influence and make the world a little bit more like his kind of world, I want to do it.

Someone may respond, "Yes, but that's not the same thing as

being a good CSR. If I work in a grocery store and a customer yells at me because we're out of prune juice, I don't see that as an example of spreading Christ's influence."

But the fact is, we *do* represent him under just such circumstances. Maybe it would be more dramatic to save a life or offer spiritual advice, but you and I are stuck with prune juice problems. Those are the kinds of needs that come our way. If we don't like that, we can always change professions, but for as long as we work in customer service, those are the kinds of problems that we'll be expected to solve.

This is where the imitation of Christ begins. If we can't at least *want* to help others, then we'll have to abandon the idea of imitating him. But to put the matter more positively, we don't have to despair of imitating him just because we aren't CSR superstars. So long as we really want to help the people who come to us with their problems, we're on the right track.

### *Questions for Reflection and Discussion*

1.  Why do you suppose Christ was so eager to heal the leper in the story?

2.  Do you think it's possible for us as CSRs to adopt Christ's attitude toward those who approach us? What difference would it make in our work if we could do this?

3.  Have you ever tried praying to be helpful before you started your shift? Could you tell whether your prayer was answered?

4. Do you recognize the significance of "prune juice problems"? Can you see that you are representing Jesus when problems like these arise? Or do you wish that you could address more dramatic issues?

# 3 MOVING MOUNTAINS

Let's return to the CSR in the previous chapter who promised to call us back by 5 P.M. Consider two scenarios, each of which gives us an alternative description of this woman:

*Scenario 1: She calls us back later that afternoon as promised, but she has bad news. Although she has spent the entire day working on our problem, she has been unable to resolve it for us. Resolution must come from the operations area, and they refuse to help. She has spoken with the vice president in charge of operations, and he insists that nothing can be done. We ask to speak to the VP ourselves, but she tells us the operations area doesn't take calls from customers. No matter what we suggest, she says she has tried it herself and failed. She sounds terribly frustrated. We can tell she really does care. But she simply cannot help us.*

*Scenario 2: She calls us back later that afternoon as*

*promised. She apologizes again for the fact that we have been inconvenienced and tells us that she has resolved the problem. As she gives us the details, we're not only satisfied but surprisingly pleased. She has done what she said she would do, and more.*

If you were the customer, which of these two women would you rather have working on your case? Wouldn't it be the lady described in Scenario 2?

I'm not going back on what I said in the previous chapter. As customers, we do want CSRs who are eager to help us. But *wanting* to help us is not enough. Effective customer service people should actually be able to help. If they can't, then it really doesn't matter how badly they want to do so. With a sigh, we'll ask to speak to someone who *can* help us.

As you and I know firsthand, however, that's one of the difficult things about doing customer service work. In fact, that's another reason why so many of us lose our natural desire to help our customers. Again and again we try to do the right thing but fail. The people who have the authority to solve the problem are often unable or unwilling to do anything about it. Disappointed, we eventually stop making promises we know we can't keep. What seems to the customer like a lack of interest is actually a lack of faith—in the system, that is. We don't believe we can help, so we don't try.

The point I want to emphasize is that this truly is a lack of faith. Yes, we've tried and failed. But most of us can't say we've tried everything. Most of us haven't tried it Jesus' way.

### *Christ as a Doer of the Impossible*

The people who meet Christ in the New Testament gospels are amazed at his power. They ask, "What sort of man is this, that even the wind and sea obey him?" (Matthew 8:27). On another occasion, the people "were all amazed, and kept saying to one another, 'What kind of utterance is this? For with authority and power he commands the unclean spirits, and out they come!'" (Luke 4:36). People are filled with wonder at the seemingly-impossible things he is able to do.

Again: "And they were astonished beyond measure, saying, 'He has done everything well; he even makes the deaf to hear and the mute to speak'" (Mark 7:37). He turns water into wine, stills a tempest, and feeds thousands of people from the contents of a little boy's lunchbox. "We have never seen anything like this!" people say—and they're right (Mark 2:12).

But it's not supposed to stop with him. He tells his disciples that what he does, they should do, too:

*Very truly, I tell you, the one who believes in me will also do the works that I do and, in fact, will do greater works than these, because I am going to the Father. I will do whatever you ask in my name, so that the Father may be glorified in the Son. If in my name you ask me for anything, I will do it (John 14:12-14).*

He lists a variety of powers that his followers will be granted (Mark 16:17-18). He sends out his closest disciples with this mandate: "Cure the sick, raise the dead, cleanse the lepers, cast out demons" (Matthew 10:8).

## *Miracles as the Norm*

But the disciples are just as amazed as the people in the crowd. Jesus repeatedly expresses dismay at his disciples' lack of faith. "Do you not yet understand?" (Mark 8:21).

The gospels describe a head-on clash between life as we know it and life as Christ says it ought to be. The disciples are shocked when he walks on water. They can't imagine how he can feed thousands of people in the desert. They're amazed at his power just as we would be amazed today if someone were to perform such feats like these. To us, such things would be considered extraordinary.

But Christ doesn't share this assessment. He calls his disciples "hard of heart" and "slow to understand." He shakes his head and says, "O ye of little faith." What the disciples consider extraordinary, Christ considers the norm. He represents life as it ought to be, and he doesn't understand why we would be willing to live any other way. He doesn't say, "I know this is all quite incredible, but you've got to try to believe." Instead, he says, "Repent and believe."

The New Testament gospels do not present us only with a gentle sage who teaches people to be kind to each other. Nor do they portray Christ merely as the savior of souls. The gospels also describe Christ as One who has come to make the world a better place. He isn't timid about using his power to help others, and he has little patience for people who don't share his sense of mission.

While everyone around him marvels at his power, he marvels at people's lack of faith. In fact, his own ability to perform miracles depends greatly on the faith of his beneficiaries. Sometimes he is unable to do much, because people don't believe. He finds this incredible.

### *What This Means for Us*

Have you ever wondered what kinds of miracles you and I, as followers of Christ, are expected to perform today? What opportunities do we have to continue Christ's work of blessing and caring in this day and time? I don't know about other people, but we CSRs are often asked to perform miracles. Here's what it sounds like when that happens:

*I've talked to five people and none of them could help me. Can you?*

That's *our* invitation to work wonders. Nobody has ever approached me asking to be healed, but people ask me to perform customer service miracles every day. When that happens, I can't just shrug and say, "I'm not a miracle worker." As a follower of Jesus, I don't have that luxury. *I* may not be out to save the world but *Jesus* is, and his plan includes me. He'll never hold it against me that I didn't heal anybody, but he does expect me to perform the kinds of miracles that are appropriate within my own vocation. And for me, that means solving the seemingly-impossible problems that my customers bring my way.

It comes down to this. I said in the last chapter that the CSR's imitation of Christ begins with our willingness to help others as Christ himself did. But this is the next step: any CSR who wants to imitate Christ must believe in miracles. More than that: we must *rely* on miracles, expecting that we will be empowered to do what's right for our customers even when huge obstacles stand in the way. If God has called us to be in this place at this time, then God will help us to do what's right. And if that means that a mountain has to be moved, then you and I are now in the mountain-moving business. Say your prayers and grab a shovel.

## *Questions for Reflection and Discussion*

1. As long as we care about the customer, what does it matter if we're unable to help?

2. Why does Christ expect us to believe in the seemingly-impossible? What's so virtuous about exercising faith?

3. Someone might object that the miracles in the New Testament gospels have nothing to do with our performance of our daily work. What do you think? Are we responsible for carrying on Christ's works of wonder? And if so, is our employment one of the means by which

we're expected to do it?

4. Perhaps you've come up against brick walls before as a CSR. Can you describe the obstacles you faced? What do you think could have been done about them?

# 4 A NEW KIND OF LISTENING

Our task, then, is not only to be kind and caring but to move mountains in Jesus' name. If you've been a CSR for very long, however, then you know how hard it can be to get things done for your customers. It's one thing to believe in moving mountains and quite another thing to move them. How do we get started?

The answer might surprise you. For CSRs who practice the imitation of Christ, the moving of mountains begins with a new kind of listening, a kind they didn't teach us in CSR training.

### *What They Taught Us*

Our trainers may have called it Active Listening, but let's be honest. "Active Listening" (also called "Empathic Listening") was originally developed for use in counseling and conflict resolution. It's a powerful tool that helps us put aside our prejudices and really hear what other people are saying, even if they're saying things we don't want to hear. True "Active Listening" is all about letting the other person talk, and when *we* finally get *our* chance, we're supposed to mirror back what we hear *them* saying.

What they taught us in CSR training wasn't anything like that. We work in a fast-paced environment, and there's no time for heart-to-heart discussions. And why should there be? The goal of Active Listening is to open us up to a much deeper level of interaction than we're used to. Why would we want to do that in a commercial environment? So let's stop pretending that CSRs engage in Active Listening. It would be more accurate to say that we were taught to practice "the CSR Conversation."

When we have CSR Conversations, we don't just passively absorb what our customers say. Instead, we maintain control of the discussion, guiding our clients as quickly as possible to the point at issue and keeping them on the subject if they begin to stray. We ask probing questions to discover if our clients forgot to tell us anything important. Once we have all the information we need, we answer their questions or solve their problems. Then we bring the conversation to a polite but timely close so that we can turn our attention to the next customer. Trainers like to call this "Active Listening" because we do listen to our customers, but not passively. From our first words of greeting, we're taking action—trying to get at the heart of the problem and solving it.

The CSR Conversation has a number of good features. It provides focus to our customer encounters rather than letting them meander. It encourages us to anticipate our clients' needs and equips us with questions to help clarify what we're being asked to do. It prompts us to notice when our customers appear hesitant or confused about what we have told them, or to recognize that they have other questions they don't know how to put into words.

All of this is great. In fact, we need to be *at least* this attentive to our customers if we want to imitate Christ, for he, too, asks probing questions even when he already knows the answers. For example, on Resurrection Sunday two of his followers leave Jerusalem all upset about the rumors that he's alive (Luke 24:13-32). As they walk along the road out of the city, they have an animated discussion and Jesus—the very person they're talking about—quietly joins them.

He doesn't clear his throat and interrupt: "Hell-*o-o-o-o*! It's me. Don't you get it?" Instead, he asks them what they're talking about.

They get annoyed at him, because they think he's out of the loop. "You must be the only one in town who doesn't know what's going on," they tell him.

He shrugs. "So? What's going on?" (I'm paraphrasing here, in case you're wondering.)

And out it comes: the story of Christ's death and resurrection and their feelings about it all. Jesus lets them talk it out, and only then does he reason with them. He still doesn't tell them who he is, because they need some time to work through it. He could say, "Look. I'm alive. See? Get over it. *Next!*" But he takes time to talk with them. He guides them step-by-step.

So the CSR Conversation has at least this much going for it.

Even though it's designed for a commercial environment, it does encourage us to be like Jesus to that extent. Imitating Christ requires that we give our customers *at least* the level of attention that a good CSR Conversation dictates.

But, as I said in the previous chapter, imitating Christ also means moving mountains when necessary. And in order to do *that*, we need to practice a new kind of listening. The CSR Conversation is a two-way discussion, but if we want to imitate Christ, we've got to develop the art of the Three-Way.

### Say What?

Let's forget that we're CSRs for a moment. If we want to be like Christ, then we must learn to receive direction from God. Christ himself was (to put it mildly) extremely good at doing what his Father wanted. "[N]ot my will, but yours be done," he said (Luke 22:42), "not what I want, but what you want" (Mark 14:36). And he encouraged his disciples to make that wish the focus of their daily prayer life: "Thy kingdom come. Thy will be done, on earth as it is in heaven" (Matthew 6:10 KJV).

But how do we find out what God wants from us?

"Listen!" Jesus replies (Mark 4:3). And his Father agrees: "This is my Son, the Beloved; with him I am well pleased; listen to him!" (Matthew 17:5). Christ says many times: "Whoever has ears to hear, let him hear" (Mark 4:9,23; Matthew 11:15; 13:9,43; Luke 8:8; 14:35).

These, of course, are metaphors. If we try to take them

literally, sitting very still with our eyes closed, something like this might result: we'll hear a barking dog, a distant siren, the rustling of a breeze through the trees, children playing... and then the sound of our own snoring. That's not what he means when he says, "Listen."

First of all, he means to take his teachings very seriously. Don't just frame them and hang them on your wall. Study them. Pray to understand them. Discuss them with other disciples. Think long and hard about them. And most importantly, *do* them. "Pay attention to what you hear," Christ says, and he adds: "the measure you give will be the measure you get, and still more will be given to you" (Mark 4:24). If we do what he teaches us, we'll get better at listening.

"Everyone then who hears these words of mine and acts on them will be like a wise man who built his house on rock," says the Master. "And everyone who hears these words of mine and does not act on them will be like a foolish man who built his house on sand" (Matthew 7:24, 26). This metaphor about "hearing" therefore means to learn Jesus' teachings and to *do* them.

The second part should come naturally. If we're studying his sayings and trying to act on them, then we'll automatically ask, "How do they apply to *this* situation?" That's where the metaphor of listening becomes especially relevant, because it's not often clear how Christ's general principles apply to any one particular case. So we pray for specific guidance and we watch for clues, then we do what we think God is asking us to do in each case. Will

31

we make mistakes? Absolutely! But we keep trying, because that's what it means to be an imitator of Christ. "My sheep hear my voice," he says (John 10:27). The message may get a little garbled sometimes, but we keep listening and doing our best to follow.

Jesus has complete confidence in us, despite our mistakes. When he says, "Whoever has ears to hear, let him hear," he's affirming that God *is* trying to tell us something and that we *can* receive God's message if we tune our ears (by which he actually means our minds and hearts).

Of course, all of this listening and doing takes place amidst our daily activities. We don't listen for God just in the morning before we start our day, or kneeling beside our bed at night. We're supposed to be listening and watching for God's messages to us throughout the day and responding to them as we receive them on-the-fly. The New Testament tells us to "pray without ceasing... for this is the will of God in Christ Jesus for you" (I Thessalonians 5:17-18). In moments of quiet meditation we practice our ability to listen without distractions, but we're also expected to keep listening even when we're doing other things. I'm not saying it's easy, but it *is* part of being his disciple.

This means we must listen for God's voice even when we're in the middle of a conversation. In fact, we must get into the habit of considering all of our conversations Three-Ways. While we talk with another person—no matter what it's about—we should continue to be attentive to the voice of God as well. Sometimes we'll discover God giving us suggestions about how to reply.

Other times we may find that God is speaking to us through that person. It can take many shapes and forms, but all two-way interactions are really Three-Ways for us, because everything we do and say is part of our lifelong communication with God.

### *The Three-Way CSR Conversation*

Now we're ready to examine how this affects us in our roles as CSRs. What difference would it make if we were deliberate about having Three-Way *CSR* Conversations?

First, it would change our perspective. Especially if we work in a call center, we're constantly aware that a Quality Manager may be monitoring us. We expend a lot of energy trying to get a good score: using the customer's name the required number of times, following the appropriate script, and so on. But if we realize that all of our customer interactions are Three-Ways, then that means that Somebody Else is listening, too. Suddenly it's about more than just getting a good score. Now the focus is on serving people in Jesus' name. While we acknowledge our responsibility to use company scripting, we become intent on doing more than that. We aim to bless and help others: something the script only hints at.

Second, a Three-Way CSR Conversation puts us in touch with resources that a two-way does not. A Three-Way isn't just a conversation—it's a prayer. We're waiting on our customers and praying for them, all at the same time. Talk about multi-tasking! In effect, we're asking for God's blessing on our customers *and*

33

making ourselves available as the vehicle through which that blessing can come. We do what we can, but sometimes that's not enough. We may not have the answers or the right tools, but in a Three-Way we reach out to Someone whose knowledge and power exceed our own.

Third, a Three-Way slowly transforms us into disciples of the risen Christ. For example, any Three-Way Conversation (whether on or off the job) requires us to have the highest respect for others, to want the best for them, to listen without judging, and so on. A Three-Way is a constant reminder to live by Jesus' teachings, because we're talking to God while we're conversing with others. The neat thing about a Three-Way *CSR* conversation is that we're practicing our faith *through our daily work*. We're becoming the kind of people God wants us to be precisely by engaging in the Three-Way CSR Conversation, because we're doing what we're paid to do—but we're doing it with God.

In all these respects, a Three-Way CSR Conversation is quite different from the way we normally talk to our customers. It's our attempt at hearing God's call and heeding it even in the gritty world of commercial transactions. In the next few chapters I'll explain in more detail how it works, but for now I want to emphasize this: we can't imitate Christ without the Spirit's help. We open ourselves up to that help by praying about everything, even while it's happening. We don't just live *for* Christ—we live *with* him. The Three-Way CSR Conversation is how we do that.

## *Questions for Reflection and Discussion*

1. Do you think my description of "The CSR Conversation" is accurate? Is that how you were trained to speak to your customers? Have you modified the technique in ways that suit your personality? Give examples.

2. Do you agree that something more than the CSR Conversation is needed if we're going to imitate Christ on the job? Why or why not?

3. You may not have referred to it as a Three-Way, but have you tried to discern the will of God in concrete situations? Can you identify moments when you believe you were successful? What do you base your belief on?

4. Do you agree that a Three-Way CSR Conversation would be quite different from the way we CSRs normally do our jobs? Why or why not?

# 5 CSR... OR JUDGE AND JURY?

I said in the previous chapter that a Three-Way CSR Conversation makes us strive to follow Jesus' teachings, and one of those teachings is not to judge others. "Do not judge," Christ says, "and you will not be judged; do not condemn, and you will not be condemned. Forgive, and you will be forgiven" (Luke 6:37). "For with the judgment you make you will be judged, and the measure you give will be the measure you get" (Matthew 7:2). This is not optional. It's one of the main things we must attend to in our imitation of Christ. If we're communing with God throughout our day, then we'll find ourselves constantly on guard against condemning those who come to us for help.

But this will be very different from what we're used to doing, because judging is a prime occupational hazard for CSRs. Many of us do it all the time and don't even realize it. Do you disagree? Let me phrase it another way. We CSRs have a lot of pet peeves. Customers often rub us the wrong way. So we service them and then, after they're gone, we turn to our coworkers and vent. We don't think of it as judging, of course. We think we're just letting off steam. But it amounts to the same thing. I'll give you some examples.

### *Stupid Questions*

We all know the saying, "There are no stupid questions," but whoever it was who said that, he must not have been a CSR. If you've been in this business for very long, you've probably heard a lot of good candidates for "Dumbest Question Ever." I'm tempted to leave the next few pages blank and let you write in your favorites. People say the darnedest things, and for some reason they tend to reserve the best ones for us.

What do we do when we're asked a stupid question? It depends on the CSR. Some of us answer it as courteously we can, trying not to laugh. Others can't help but give a withering reply. But regardless of how we respond, it's natural for us to turn to our coworkers afterwards and share the experience with them. If it's funny, we laugh. If it's not, we shake our heads in disgust. Either way, we're agreed on one thing: you and I are like Einstein compared to *that* loser.

This is perfectly understandable behavior. It's our way of getting through the day. But let's be honest: whenever we do that, we're commenting on the level of intelligence of our customers. We're not just repeating the question; we're making a blanket judgment about the person who asked it. "How could anyone be that dumb?" we ask.

I don't mean to be a killjoy, but if we're serious about imitating Christ then we should be troubled whenever we catch ourselves talking like that. Jesus' remark about this kind of behavior is chilling:

*You have heard that it was said to those of ancient times, "You shall not murder"; and "whoever murders shall be liable to judgment." But I say to you that if you are angry with a brother or sister, you will be liable to judgment; and if you insult a brother or sister, you will be liable to the council; and if you say, "You fool," you will be liable to the hell of fire (Matthew 5:21-22).*

Is it just me, or do you think he's got strong views on this subject?

Let's forget about hellfire. If we're engaged in a Three-Way CSR Conversation and somebody asks us what sounds like a stupid question, here's what ought to happen. We should feel prompted by the Spirit to ask ourselves, "Is this person a fool?" And the right answer, according to Jesus, would be No. The obvious next question should be, "Then why is he asking such a stupid question?" There are several possible reasons:

Maybe he's tired, stressed, or in a hurry, and he's not saying exactly what he means. Let's see how we can help him.

Or perhaps he's not very articulate. He messes up his words all the time. So sue him.

Or he could be asking about something we've always taken for granted and never thought to inquire about. The question seems stupid because it hasn't occurred to us before.

Or it could be that he's missing something that we think should be obvious. For example, he wants to know where the nearest copier is, and it's right behind him. Or he gets in the wrong line even though we think the lines are clearly marked. Or he pushes and pushes on the door that says, "Use other door." Those kinds of things are no-brainers for *us* because they're part of our everyday landscape, but people who are new to our environment can easily make such mistakes. It's funny to us because we can see it coming, but you and I would make similar mistakes if we were on somebody else's turf. It happens to the best of us.

There may be a number of good reasons why this person is asking what sounds like a dumb question. A Three-Way CSR Conversation invites us to discover those reasons. When we do, then we'll realize that people are a lot smarter than they seem. We just have to give them a chance.

### *Barriers to Communication*

"Foreign accents!" a CSR mutters, shaking her head. But what she's thinking is: "Why don't you learn to speak English, you [bleeping] foreigner!" She isn't just complaining about how hard it is to understand the customer. She's voicing a judgment about him. Yes, it's frustrating when language barriers prevent us from understanding our clients, but that's not what's happening here.

This CSR is implying that there's something morally blameworthy about a person having an accent. She's holding it against him that he came to this country from somewhere else.

But this criticism cuts both ways. One of the biggest gripes about customer service call centers these days is that they're staffed by people with accents. I get that a lot from my customers. "Whew," they say. "Thank God I got somebody who speaks English." And the complaint is fueled by reports that a lot of CSR jobs have been exported overseas. As soon as customers hear a CSR with a foreign accent, they get angry, assuming that their call has been transferred halfway around the world. They don't seem to realize how many "foreigners" are here in the United States, working as CSRs right along with the rest of us natural-born citizens.

Somebody needs to stop this ignorance, and you and I are prime candidates. We, at least, must never pass judgment on our callers because they don't speak like we do. And if we forget from time to time, the Spirit of God will remind us if we're practicing a lively Three-Way.

"Foreign accents!"

*[Ahem.] Remember me?*

"Oops. Sorry, Lord."

After all, communication across language barriers is part of the job of an imitator of Christ. As the second chapter of Acts shows us, the Holy Spirit has a long history of bridging such gaps.

Look again at the Parable of the Good Samaritan (Luke 10:25-

37). One of Christ's opponents asks him how to inherit eternal life, and Christ turns the question back on the questioner. The man says that two commandments are most important: to love God and to love your neighbor as yourself. "And who is my neighbor?" the man asks him. To answer this question, Jesus tells the story of the Samaritan who helped a Jewish person in an emergency. The Jews have a lot of good reasons to hate the Samaritans, but Jesus tells this story on purpose. "Go and do likewise," he says. If you're going to be an imitator of Christ, then from now on you're everybody's neighbor. Stop griping about their accents. Stop sneering at the color of their skin. The Good Samaritan overlooked such distinctions. "Go and do likewise."

But accents aren't the only barrier to communication. Some customers mumble, others screech. Some talk too fast, others too slow. We're never happy. Remember, however, that these are the kinds of things customers dislike about *us*, too. We may be quick to pick up on their quirks, but they pick up on ours just as much.

Speaker phones are another pet peeve of CSRs who work in call centers. Customers don't realize it, but it's hard for us to hear them when they use a speaker phone. In some call centers, it's against department policy to carry on a conversation with a client under those circumstances. But our irritation goes way beyond what's warranted. We tend to get mad at people just for doing it.

What we say is: "Can you please take me off speaker phone?"

What we mean is: "Take me off speaker, you idiot!"

It's all the same thing, whether they have an accent or a speech impediment, whether they have us on speaker or we have a bad phone connection. One way or the other, the customer is inconveniencing us, and we don't like to be inconvenienced. So what do we do? We get mad at the customer. But a Three-Way CSR Conversation helps us to get over it.

### Special Requests

You're a checker in a supermarket and a customer wants to use two coupons for the same item. You don't think she's allowed to do that, but she points out that there isn't any verbiage on either coupon saying she can't. You've got a long line of customers and they're getting impatient. You're the bad guy no matter what you do. As you page your manager, you shake your head. *Why do they have to make it so difficult?*

Most of us CSRs are not like the employees at Burger King®: special orders *do* upset us. When customers ask us to do things that are out of the ordinary, we become annoyed. And we have good reason for feeling that way, because our customers are asking us to do things that seem to be outside company guidelines.

Again, let's be honest. When we get special requests, we don't just grumble. We pass judgment on the person making the request. "People always want something for nothing," we say.

If we're having a Three-Way CSR Conversation, however, the Spirit of God just might remind us of Christ's words about a much tougher case: "[I]f anyone forces you to go one mile, go also the second mile" (Matthew 5:41). That sounds like management, doesn't it? They talk glibly about going the second mile for the customer. But it didn't start out as a management slogan. Jesus said it first, and we see him doing it a lot in the gospels.

Christ's disciples are constantly bombarded with special requests. Parents want Jesus to touch their children (Mark 10:13-16). "What, are you kidding?" the disciples reply. "He doesn't have time to admire your babies. Don't you realize who he is?"

They catch a guy they never met before, healing people in the name of Jesus (Mark 9:39-40). "You can't do that!" they tell him. "You're not authorized to use the brand name!"

A woman requests healing for her child, and she's very persistent (Mark 7:24-30). She's not Jewish, though, so they think she has no right to bother the Master. "Lord, this lady won't leave us alone! Can you get rid of her?"

In each case, the disciples have excellent reasons for assuming that the request can't be granted. But in each case, they're wrong.

Sometimes even the crowd gets upset about a special order. Christ is on his way to Jerusalem to die on the cross (Mark 10:46-52). There's an air of solemnity as he makes his way through the city of Jericho. On the outskirts of town, people watch him go. They may not understand what's happening, but they know it's serious. Then some blind beggar finds out that Jesus has passed by, and he starts shouting and creating a fuss. "Wait! Come back! Have mercy on me!"

"Be quiet," people say. "He's got his own problems. Show some respect."

But the blind man yells louder. He's like a customer who just found out there was a big sale and he missed it. He loudly insists on speaking to the manager, but all the other customers just want him to shut up.

Jesus stops. The people sigh with relief and tell the blind man, "All right, it's okay. Go on, he's calling for you."

The blind man feels his way to the front of the crowd and Jesus asks him, "What do you want me to do for you?" And he gives the man what he wants. Jesus isn't put out, even though everybody else is.

Sometimes Christ himself initiates an outrageous request. He has just finished teaching a crowd of thousands, and it's late in the afternoon (Mark 6:35-37). The disciples suggest that they call it a day so the people can get back to town and eat.

"Why don't *you* feed them?" Christ replies.

You can imagine what the disciples say about that!

There are, of course, lots of customers who ask for things they can't have. A lady who's new to our store whines because her neighbor, who shops regularly with us, received something in the mail promising a freebie if she opened an XYZ account. "Why didn't I get the same deal?" she asks. Or a guy in his 30s complains about a product we offer that targets people over 50. "That's age discrimination," he claims. "You have to give me the same benefit."

In cases like these we can't do what they ask, no matter how much they scream and yell about it. But we're so busy bracing ourselves for *those* kinds of encounters that we tend to play the role of judge and jury first, CSR second. If we're too quick to reject special requests, we may fail to recognize legitimate ones. And that's how customers fall between the cracks, because some of them have real problems but nobody in our company steps up to help.

### *So...*

Now do you understand why I said that judging is an occupational hazard for CSRs? If we're not careful, we could easily spend our entire workday griping about our clients. A Three-Way CSR Conversation helps us avoid doing that. It reminds us not to condemn our customers and presents us with positive alternatives to judging them. It's the Holy Spirit's way of guiding us through the difficult terrain of customer service work.

But can a Three-Way help us when we need the greatest help of all? Can it aid us in dealing constructively with our most difficult customers? That will be the subject of the next chapter.

### *Questions for Reflection and Discussion*

1. What's so bad about judging people? Do you agree that it's an occupational hazard for CSRs? Why or why not?

2. What difference would it make if we consciously practiced a Three-Way every time someone asked us a stupid question?

3. Do you believe that the imitation of Christ can help us

overcome communication barriers? Are you willing to give it a try?

4.  Why do you think Christ's disciples were so quick to reject special requests? And why was Christ so receptive to such requests?

# 6 THE CUSTOMER FROM HELL

Our heart races. Our face is hot. We can feel the veins tightening in our neck. A million thoughts cross our mind and yet, ironically, we're not thinking at all. We're way past thinking. All we want to do is lash out at this person.

"No!" we want to reply. "*You* listen to *me!*"

Or:

"You can *have* my job, sir. But you won't like it any better than I do!"

Or:

"Don't blame me. I don't make the rules. I just work here."

Dealing with difficult customers is one of the hardest aspects of being a CSR. People scream and yell, they call us names, they insult us, and we're supposed to let it roll off our backs.

Management offers advice: "Whenever a customer swears at you, pretend they're saying 'pumpkin.' Then concentrate on counting the pumpkins. It's fun and it takes your mind off the fact that they're swearing at you." Or: "Apologize. An apology is not an admission of error and it helps calm the customer down." Some of this advice is useful, some not. But if you're like me, it's hard to remember hints and tips when your blood's boiling.

This is where the imitation of Christ becomes especially helpful. We may survive these challenging moments by using clever devices, but Christ offers much more than that. He gives us a point of view that totally transforms the nature of these encounters. Instead of reacting to irate customers, he teaches us to act purposefully toward all of them, including the angry ones.

### The Big Picture

We've been talking about the imitation of Christ in piecemeal fashion, but now it's time to look at the larger vision. For our purposes, that vision can be summed up this way: Christ came to bless people, heal them, minister to them, and free them from bondage of every kind. In a word, his mandate was to bring God's love to all people. And that's our mandate, too, if we're committed to imitating him.

But the Greek word for love that recurs throughout Jesus' teachings is significant: it's *agape* (pronounced uh-GAH-pay). I say it's significant because of what the word does *not* mean. This word is *not* used to describe the kind of affection that we feel toward our close friends and family. The Greeks had another word for that: it was *philia* (fill-EE-ah). I'm willing to bet that *philia* is what most of us have in mind when we think of the word "love."

It's the warm fuzzy feeling we get when we're reminded of the people we're close to. We'd do anything for them. We enjoy being with them. They light up our world. And therefore we'll overlook their shortcomings. If our nephew kicks us in the shins, we may not like it very much, but we won't stop loving him.

The kind of love Jesus talks about isn't like that. It doesn't come naturally. If a complete stranger were to kick us in the shins, we wouldn't feel the love. Christ is talking about a different approach. *Agape* isn't a feeling, or at least it doesn't start out as one. The love Jesus talks about is deliberate. It's a matter of principle. As followers of Christ, we're determined to treat all people like family, even though we don't have the same emotional investment in them that we have in our real family and friends. *Agape* is a commitment to widening the circle of our concern, a commitment to caring about people who lie outside our sphere of personal interest. It isn't automatic. We have to practice thinking and acting that way.

But there's more. We aren't just committed to caring passively about people: we're also committed to putting our caring into action—to helping those who need help (Matthew 25:31-46). If they're hungry, we'll feed them. If they're thirsty, we'll give them something to drink. If they're in prison (either literally or figuratively), we'll visit them. And if we can help anyone find a better life—even in some small way—we'll celebrate.

You're probably familiar with Christ's parable of the Prodigal Son (Luke 15:11-32). A young man coerces his dad into giving him his inheritance early, and then he moves to the big city and blows all his money in hedonistic pursuits. He returns home penniless and ashamed. But Dad doesn't rub it in. He runs out to greet his son, welcomes him back effusively, and even throws a party for him.

Everybody knows this much of the story, but a lot of people aren't familiar with the ending, and that's the most important part. There's another son, and when he comes in from the fields to see that his dad is throwing a party for his sibling, he becomes furious. He wants to see his brother punished for his mistakes, not rewarded. His dad tries to explain, but the self-righteous son feels personally insulted.

This story spells out the situation quite clearly: Jesus is in the blessing business, and whenever he succeeds at it, he celebrates. Like the other son in the parable, however, the religious leaders are intent upon cursing and accusing in the name of God. We're all like that, to some extent. We identify certain kinds of people as the bad guys, and we hope they'll get what's coming to them. But Christ says that's not what God is all about. God isn't gunning for bad guys. God wants to bless everybody. *Everybody*. Unconditionally. And Christ wants to work through us to make it happen.

### Take That... and That

That's the big picture, but what's this got to do with the Customer from Hell? Simply this: if we're committed to the imitation of Christ, then *his* focus should be *our* focus. As we're waiting on each customer, we should be engaged in a lively Three-Way CSR Conversation, and in each case our underlying prayer should be, "Lord, how can you and I bless this person?" It shouldn't matter to us whether they're naughty or nice—we should want to bless all of them, especially those who seem disgruntled. If they're upset, we should want to help.

Jesus says, "…bless those who curse you" (Luke 6:28). The average person in the pew may not have much chance to practice this maxim, but you and I have opportunities every day. As CSRs, we get cursed out just for saying hello. Lucky us! It's not something we look forward to, of course, but it does give us a unique way of imitating Christ.

What happens next depends on whether we're in touch with God through a Three-Way. If we are, then the Spirit will prompt us to do what Jesus says: "Bless those who curse you." In practical terms, that means to listen carefully to discern what this person needs from us.

Anger, they say, is a secondary emotion. If people are angry, then it's because they're experiencing something bad. They're frustrated, or their feelings have been hurt, or they're afraid, or they're in pain. They could have a toothache or maybe their shoes are too tight. I don't mean to belittle anger, but it's usually more productive to get past it and to solve whatever problem has caused the anger in the first place.

So when a customer yells at us, we should ask God, *Why is*

*this person so upset? And what can we do to bless them in this moment?* Then we should get down to work, gently asking the questions that will help us get to the root of the problem.

You may object to this: "Are we just supposed to let customers beat up on us?" After all, a fuller reading of the passage says: "Love your enemies, do good to those who hate you, bless those who curse you, pray for those who abuse you. If anyone strikes you on the cheek, offer the other also. . ." (Luke 6:27-29).

We may imagine customers bludgeoning us: "Take *that*... and *that*... and *that*," while we just sit there and let them do it. But that's not what Christ is saying. He's not asking us to be wimps. He just wants us to remain open and receptive to others rather than getting defensive. And we *will* be open to them if we want to bless them as badly as he does.

The ending of that passage is significant: "But love your enemies, do good, and lend, expecting nothing in return. Your reward will be great, and you will be children of the Most High; for he is kind to the ungrateful and the wicked. Be merciful, just as your Father is merciful" (Luke 6:35-36). *That's* why we're kind to people who are unkind to us—not because we're cowards or saps. We do it because *God* "is kind to the ungrateful and the wicked," and we aspire to be like our Father.

Here's where I'm going with this. When a customer comes out swinging, we can sit there and say, "One pumpkin, two pumpkin, three pumpkin," or we can turn to God in our ongoing Three-Way and ask, "How can I bless this person?" In the first case, we're using a gimmick to help us remain calm. In the second case, we're falling back on what we try to do all the time: we're working together with God to make the world a better place.

### The Hard Cases

Watch what Jesus does in the gospels. He takes the hard cases: the seemingly incurable; the people who have been written off as hopeless. And he deals with some tough customers: crazy people who scream and yell and get violent. Some of them really *are* from hell.

Let me say something about that before we go on. The gospels are full of stories about people possessed by demons, and in every case Jesus casts the demons out of them. In our role as CSRs, you and I come in contact with lots of hysterical people, but we don't have that option. I keep talking about the imitation of Christ, but don't get me wrong. I don't recommend that you perform exorcisms on irate customers. You and I aren't divine, after all. But there is something we can do that mimics Christ's work.

On one occasion he's confronted by a man possessed by a host of devils (Mark 5:1-20). This guy lives in the wild because he's too dangerous to be around others. He scratches and tears at himself, so he wears chains to minimize the damage he can do to his own body. Christ frees him from those demons, and after they're gone the text says something very interesting: it tells us the man is "sitting there, clothed and in his right mind" (v. 15).

You and I may not have the power to rid people of their

demons, but we can help them get back in their right mind.

I once spoke with a customer who was verbally abusive from the very beginning of the call. I ignored his insults, and I quickly realized that he had a legitimate complaint. I knew what to do, but it would take a few days for the correction to be reflected on his account. I apologized for his inconvenience and told him what I was going to do about it. I explained how long it was going to take and promised him that, when the problem was resolved, I would call him back. He was still grumpy and skeptical when the conversation finished, but the white heat of his anger had at least cooled.

A few days later, I called him back and reported that the correction had been made. I'll never forget his reaction when I apologized again for his inconvenience. He said, "Well, but it gave me a chance to meet *you*. You said what you was gonna do, and you did what you said." He sounded like he was fighting back tears. Some customers are like that: they can't control their emotions. If they're mad, they express their anger violently. If we placate them, they sound almost repentant. I feel sorry for them. But that's where we want to end up as CSRs: helping such people get back "into their right mind," even if they come to us foaming at the mouth.

### *Yes, But. . .*

You may have some objections. What if we can't help them? For example, what if their demands are unreasonable? Suppose a customer insists on getting her money back, but she broke the product by treating it in an inappropriate manner. Our managers say we can't give her the refund, but she keeps on screaming at us and won't back down. What are we supposed to do?

The answer may seem inadequate, but here it is: kindly refuse. The key word here is "kindly." Treat her like you'd treat your own child who's having a tantrum: don't give in to her, but don't fight back, either. Just remain calm and accepting. You will be blessing her more than you realize. Many people don't know what it's like to be accepted for who they are. In Jesus' name, commit yourself to offering that quiet acceptance, and that in itself will be a gift to your customers—even those who are ungrateful.

Here's a tougher objection: what if the customer is evil? You may grin, but I'm serious. When I was a manager, I was often shouted at by people who were trying to defraud others. We were in the electronic money transfer business, and we kept tabs on individuals who used our service illegally. These individuals would call up elderly people and tell them they just won a new car or an all-expense-paid trip to Bermuda. They'd say, "All *you* have to do is pay the tax on it. Just call [the company I worked for] and use your credit card to wire me the money, and as soon as I get it, I'll send you your free gift." We had a whole team of sharp employees watching for situations like that, and when we identified them, we refused to transfer the money. Before long, the guy would be on my phone, threatening me with a lawsuit.

How do we imitate Christ under such circumstances? We

know the person who's yelling at us has an evil intent. He wants to harm others and will scream at us if we try to stop him. How can we "bless those who curse us" in a case like that? Well, it depends on how serious we are about imitating Christ. After all, he said repeatedly that it's sick people—not healthy ones—who need a doctor (Matthew 9:12; Mark 2:17). And he's the Doctor.

The answer is the same as in the previous case: kindly refuse. Even if every fiber of our being wants to rail against him, remember that this person, too, is a child of God—someone whom Christ wants to bless. No, we cannot give in to his demands. But we also must not give in to the temptation to hate him. What he's doing is very bad indeed, but even that doesn't make him one of the bad guys—not in God's book, anyway. God wants to bless him and lead him to a better life. But even if he spurns God's advances, God loves him even now, even when he's trying to steal money from an old lady. Our job as a CSR is to say No to him, but our task as a follower of Jesus is to pray for him and show compassion on him.

Notice how Jesus treats folks who are filled with the devil. He speaks sternly to the demons themselves, but he is infinitely kind to the people whom they possess. That's how we should be, too, if we want to imitate Christ.

Of course, most of our customers aren't evil, although some of them are extremely challenging. But in dealing with our toughest clients, it's our Three-Way conversation with Christ that must guide us, not gimmicks.

One more objection: what if the customer's right? What if she's got a valid complaint, but we're not empowered to help her? For example, what if company policy dictates that we do X, but we strongly believe that X is not the right thing? I'm not just talking about a moral dilemma. What if this customer's case reveals that our company policy has not kept up with changing circumstances? Or perhaps a new product or service doesn't work the way it's supposed to. The product developers had one idea in mind, but the operations people have an entirely different interpretation. Our customers recognize the discrepancy and want it resolved.

My experience as a frontline CSR has often made me aware of such situations. It is precisely here—in the Complaints Department—that we learn firsthand what works for our customers and what doesn't. We have information that the company needs if it's going to remain in touch with its clients.

What should we CSRs do when we become aware that our customers have a legitimate complaint and that company policy needs to be changed to accommodate this complaint? We're tempted to shrug and say, "That's not my department. Send it up the ladder to corporate." But you and I know what happens when clients contact the corporate office directly: the CEO's assistant sends the issue back down to the frontline with a sticky note that says, "Deal with this." Ultimately, it's up to us. But what can we do?

I realize I've led you on a long detour, but I'm finally ready to answer the question I raised at the end of chapter 3. As CSRs who seek to follow Christ, we must be willing to move mountains. But in practical terms, how can we do that? I'll give you a detailed answer in the next chapter.

## *Questions for Reflection and Discussion*

1. Are there certain kinds of customers whom you find it difficult to deal with? Can you pinpoint what it is that upsets you about them? What can you do to overcome these feelings in the future?

2. Can you remember occasions when you were able to calm down an angry customer and get them back "in their right mind"? What did you do in those cases? Are there strategies that you have found useful in such moments?

3. Do you agree that Christ's main focus was to bless everyone, indiscriminately? Do you believe that that should also be our focus if we want to imitate Christ? Why or why not?

4. Do you find it hard to refuse customers politely? Can you think of strategies that might help? Is it useful to reflect on cases in which Christ does this? Why or why not?

# 7 NOW, ABOUT THOSE MOUNTAINS...

Your customer is unhappy. You realize she has a valid complaint, but there aren't any procedures that tell you how to help. If you worked for a large company, you'd refer her to the area that specializes in escalated issues, but your company doesn't have a department like that. It's up to you. Either you'll find a way to assist this customer or she'll fall through the cracks. What will you do?

I've said that we CSRs are asked to perform miracles and that we can't just turn away from the tough cases. But how can we proceed when we have no guidelines?

First, we practice the Three-Way CSR Conversation. This is our way of seeking direction from God while we're listening to the customer's complaint. It makes us available to God so that God can help this person through us.

Second, we seek a more productive way of viewing the problem. "Think outside the box" is an old, tired cliché, but that's what we have to do. It's a good idea for us to remember that God *dwells* outside the box, so anytime we engage in a Three-Way, we're stretching outside our own narrow point of view. Granted, we have to become mature listeners before we'll be aware of how different God's voice is from our own, but that's what we're trying to do whenever we have a Three-Way: we're trying to get outside our own preconceptions and hear what God is saying to us from Out There.

Third, we get help from others: our coworkers, our supervisors, or a senior representative in our department. In the toughest cases, it will often be necessary to contact other departments. Each situation will be different, but the general principle is true: any unusual case will probably require that we get assistance from somebody else in the company.

And this is the core of the problem, because sometimes people in other departments are not very helpful. And that can be more frustrating than any encounter with the Customer from Hell.

## *How to Get Along with People in Operations*

We CSRs can't get the job done without relying on lots of other people in a variety of back offices. They're the ones who do the actual work. We may promise our customers the moon, but we can't deliver it. Other people do that. . . or not. So if we want to make sure that our promises are fulfilled then we have to be effective at dealing with people in those other departments. Some of them are nice and some aren't, but we need them all. Without them, we're sunk. So for starters, we've got to get along with them. Even if we aren't asking them for favors, we've still got to stay on good terms with them.

Here are some rules that I've found useful for building good relationships with people in Operations. Deviate from them at your own risk.

*Assume that you're talking to an intelligent, capable person. That may not be true, but you won't get anywhere with them if you treat them like they're stupid or incompetent.

*Believe that they're just as good as you are, that they want to do the right thing just as much as you do, and that they'll help you if they can.

*Understand that they have to follow procedures. There may be lots of reasons why they can't do what you're asking them to do, or at least why they can't do it in precisely the way you want it done. Be a quick study. The better you understand their procedures, the more effective you'll be at making requests that can be granted.

*Remember to do it as a Three-Way. Pray that God will help you work together with this person to do what's right. And listen carefully, both to the other person and to God. If you do, you might learn that you're asking for something unreasonable. Be ready to change your mind as needed.

*If you're sure that you're right and they still resist, proceed with utmost respect. No matter how difficult it may be to persuade them, remember that you'll need their help again on another issue soon—today, tomorrow, or even minutes from now. If you go ballistic, you might win this battle but you'll lose the war. Each person in the back office is essential for your success. Never forget that.

### How the Back Offices Perceive Us

Here's something else to keep in mind. Remember what I said about how we CSRs are quick to judge our customers? I have news for you. . . people in other departments are equally quick to judge *us*. It's an occupational hazard, remember? The tendency to judge afflicts them just as much as it does us. Based on what I said in chapter 5, here are the obstacles we may have to face, along with recommendations for overcoming those obstacles.

(1) They may think we're asking a stupid question. Try to be patient with them, but don't sound condescending. That'll just annoy them. Address them respectfully and they just might come around.

(2) We may have to overcome a communication barrier. They may not understand what we're asking because they use a different terminology in their department from the one we're using. All we

can do is listen carefully for such communication barriers and try to speak their language.

(3) They may get upset with us for making a special request. It will be our task to convince them that we're not asking for something out of the ordinary. We're just trying to give the client their due.

(4) They might consider us the Customer from Hell. To guard against this, we'll have to remain professional, keep emotionally-charged words out of the conversation, and stick to the facts. We should keep the discussion focused on exactly what we think needs to happen, and we should always be open to alternative ways of getting it done.

As CSRs, we're the customers' advocates. Sometimes people in the back offices are annoyed by that because they're just trying to do their jobs and we're getting involved in things we don't understand as well as they do. But if *we* don't fight for our customers, who will? We just have to remember to do it in the proper spirit—approaching operations people with respect and enlisting their help in what should be a common cause.

Everything I've said so far applies to our day-to-day dealings with the back offices. But what do we do when our customers have a problem that isn't explicitly spelled out in company policy yet? Or what if we believe the policy needs to be changed? It happens. On one occasion I had a head-on collision with a very nice lady in operations. She was polite and was also a good listener. But we reached a stalemate and I couldn't figure out why.

Then I prayed about it. . .

## *An Apparently Immovable Mountain*

A customer called to complain about his auto lease bill. After listening to his story and researching his case, I discovered that we were charging him for taxes that were not required. At the beginning of his lease, he had lived in Illinois, which was an Up-Front state: a state that required him to pay all his taxes in the beginning. He had recently moved to Wisconsin, which had a reciprocal agreement with all Up-Front states. As long as the customer had paid his taxes "up front," Wisconsin would not make him pay again if he happened to move there. This was an exception that our Policies and Procedures said nothing about.

I submitted a detailed request to the Lease Operations department to correct this error. I even printed and sent over information from the State of Wisconsin's website, showing conclusively that the tax was not to be assessed in this case. To my amazement, my request wasn't granted. In fact, I wasn't even given an explanation for why it was declined.

I called the person who had worked on the request. She was polite, so I tried again to tell her why I believed we should not be charging the tax. Although she didn't interrupt me, it was also clear that she wasn't going to change her mind. She told me she had to keep charging the customer and she didn't even try to explain why. She just kept saying it was policy and she had to do it that way.

When the conversation was over, I was deeply perplexed. I had given her explicit guidelines from the Wisconsin website that clearly told us what to do in this case, but she was unimpressed. She didn't refute the evidence nor did she claim that I had misinterpreted it. She simply dismissed it.

She was a nice person. If she had growled at me, I might have concluded that she was belligerent. But she was actually very patient and listened courteously to everything I said. On the other hand, I could see that there was nothing I could say that would convince her. And to add to my confusion, she didn't say anything that would help me understand why she was refusing to comply with the state's guidelines.

A day or two passed. I was sure that the customer was right, but my conversation with the woman in Lease Ops had seemed quite final.

"Lord," I asked, "what should I do?"

I was given the strong impression that I should call her again. But why? I couldn't think of any other way to state my case nor could I come up with alternative ways of asking her the question. I prayed again and continued to believe that God was encouraging me to call her back.

So I did. As I predicted, each of us just repeated the things we had said the previous day. Neither of us lost our temper but the discussion seemed like a waste of time.

Afterwards, I prayed. "Lord, why did You want me to call her back?"

The following question came to mind: What exactly did she tell you?

"Well, she kept saying, 'There's nothing I can do,' and 'My hands are tied,' but that doesn't make any sense to me. I've shown her the state's guidelines. Why does she say she can't do anything about it?" I pondered this. Out of all the people in the company, she was the only one who worked on taxation issues for auto leases. There wasn't anyone else *but* her who could do something about it.

Then I remembered something else she had said: "I can't change company policy." The more I thought about it, the more sense it made. Although she was the only person in a position to correct the error, she was not empowered to do so without a policy change. She could readily see that, according to the state's website, Wisconsin did not require her to continue charging this customer the tax, but it was bank policy for us to do it this way and she didn't have the authority to change the policy.

To me, it seemed like a simple thing. I had already given her the information she needed. It only remained for her to take that information to her supervisor (the man who did have the power to change our policy) and convince him to make the correction. But she didn't believe it was part of her role to make requests like that. She seemed to realize that a policy revision was called for, but she lacked the power to make it happen.

"Lord," I asked, "what can I do to help her?"

I remembered something else she had said—something about

needing a directive from the state. That had confused me, because I had already given her the guidelines from the government website. But she said that she needed "a directive."

"I get it now," I prayed. "She's telling me she won't bring this to her supervisor unless she gets something directly from the state *telling* her to do it. But how's *that* going to happen?"

My team leader didn't like getting involved in situations like this, but coincidentally she was out of the office that day and the person covering for her was the leader of our escalation unit—the area that specialized in problems like these. I discussed the situation with her and she did something my regular team leader would never have done: she gave me authorization (and time off the phones) to call the State of Wisconsin Taxation Department for advice.

The specialist who answered my call was surprisingly helpful. (Sorry, but I had a mental image of a bureaucrat who didn't want to be bothered. I was wrong.) He listened attentively and confirmed that our bank should not be assessing the tax. But now came the crucial step: I took a deep breath and asked him if he would be willing to put that in writing.

"He won't go for it, Lord."

To my amazement, he said, "I'll be glad to write you a letter." And he did. A few days later I received it: a clear statement that our bank should not be assessing the tax, along with a paragraph explaining why.

I showed it to the supervisor of the escalation group and she gave me a high five. Then I delivered it personally to the lady in Lease Ops. She glanced at the letter and said, "Thank you. *Now* I can do something."

The error was corrected on the customer's account, but more importantly, the policy was changed. In fact, the Lease Ops supervisor did the right thing: he investigated the issue thoroughly and discovered that there were several other states that engaged in this give-and-take arrangement. This resulted in a sweeping policy revision that encompassed all those reciprocal agreements and affected a lot of customers. Our CSR manuals were kept in three-ring binders (yes, we were low-tech in those days) and it was an awesome experience for me when our managers told us to rip out those pages and insert the new version.

Mission Accomplished: Mountain Moved.

## We're Only as Effective as Our Network

Despite these challenges (or perhaps because of them), this is a part of the job that I've always found especially rewarding. The Lease Ops woman I just told you about became a friend of mine after that. I made a lot of friends throughout the company in a wide variety of departments. I had to, but it wasn't *just* because I had to. It was a pleasure working with them and especially realizing that there were so many good people in other areas of the bank.

This is a fact of life for frontline CSRs. We're the ones who talk to the customers and discover the problems, but we don't do the back-office work that resolves those problems. We depend on people in other departments to do that. Sometimes it doesn't happen on its own so we have to get involved. But the resolution still isn't ours to achieve; it's theirs. That's just a result of the division of labor. But there's also a larger principle at work here— one that goes way beyond the company flow chart. It's at the heart of the imitation of Christ.

We can't save the world by ourselves, no matter how much faith we have. God may be working through us, but not *just* us. It's all about teamwork. Nor is that an accident. It's part of the plan. God is trying to save the world by reaching people like you and me *in* the world and transforming it from the inside out. Jesus gathered working people around him and shared the plan with them, and they spread the word to working people all over the world. The imitation of Christ is not a solitary pursuit. It's been a team sport from the beginning and will continue to be that way right up to the end. That's the plan.

Depending on others can be difficult at times, but that's how we perform miracles for our customers. And it's a daily reminder to us that, even within our own organization, there may be lots of other people who are just as service-oriented as we are. It can be quite inspiring to realize that we're part of a network of caring individuals. It's worth being a CSR just to experience that.

## *Questions for Reflection and Discussion*

1. Is it ever a challenge for you to communicate with people in other departments? Are there specific individuals who

are harder to get along with than others? Can you identify precisely what the problem is and how it might be resolved?

2. Do you understand why employees in the operations areas sometimes cringe when they receive calls from CSRs? What can we do to put them at ease?

3. Have you tried practicing a Three-Way when you're talking to people in other areas of your company? Can you see why it would be helpful to pray for guidance about interdepartmental conversations? Why or why not?

4. Do you agree that God's transformation of the world has been "a team sport from the beginning and will continue to be that way right up to the end"? Does that shape the way you think about people in other departments? Can you be specific?

# 8 THE OTHER LINE MOVES FASTER

You may be thinking, *All this talk about performing miracles for the customer is unrealistic and even irresponsible when we consider the people next in line. How can we aspire to such heights when our Number One Job is to move 'em in and move 'em out?*

This is the irony: that our clients want exceptional service but they also want it fast. How can we provide the level of care I've been talking about and still stay within our time constraints? Again, the answer is the imitation of Christ. He's a model for us even in this respect. He was not only perpetually giving but also remained calm when there was a long line of people waiting.

### I'll Serve Whoever's Next

Three of the four gospels tell a story that has important things to say about this subject. Mark's version is best for our purposes (Mark 5:21-43) but it can also be found in Matthew 9:18-35 and Luke 8:40-56. (I'm paraphrasing the dialogue.)

Christ and his disciples have just arrived by boat and the crowd is waiting for them. One of the leaders of the local synagogue pushes his way forward: a man named Jairus. He's what we would consider one of our best customers. With his high social status, we CSRs would serve him promptly and we'd do whatever he asked without hesitation.

But there's even more reason why we'd hustle to help him today: he's in great distress. As he rushes toward Jesus he doesn't do it as a VIP but as a father in need. "It's my little girl!" he says. "She's terribly sick! Please! Come and save her!"

Jesus goes with him, but they can only inch along down the street because of the crowds. Jairus is frustrated. His child is dying. Don't these people understand? Why don't they step aside?

Jairus and the Master burrow through the sea of onlookers, with the Twelve close behind. They inch forward, step by step by step by step by step. . .

Suddenly Jesus pauses and looks at the people behind him. Everyone else stops, too. Jairus whirls around to see what's happening.

Christ calls out to the crowd. "Who touched my clothes?"

His disciples laugh. "You're kidding, right? People are bumping into us right and left. Do you seriously want to know who touched you?"

But he keeps looking intently at the faces of the people behind him.

Finally a woman steps forward. She seems terrified and elated all at the same time. "It was me, Lord." She bows down before him and tells her story. For the past twelve years she's had a bloody discharge that won't stop. She's visited one doctor after another and gone through a series of painful procedures. Her money's gone, and after all the trouble she's been through, she's no better off than she was before. She doesn't bother to tell Jesus that she's also been an outcast all these years because her bloody discharge is condemned by the law of Moses (Leviticus 15:19-33). She doesn't need to say that. Everybody understands.

She bows her head even lower and tells him, "I thought that maybe if I could touch your clothes. . . I wouldn't have to bother you. . . just reach out to you as you passed by."

She looks up into his eyes. "So that's what I did. And I was healed. Instantly! I tried to get away, and that's when you called to me."

Jesus looks down at her tenderly. "Daughter," he says. Not *woman*, but *daughter*. She's like his own child, and he can't let her leave without telling her so. As far as anybody else is concerned, she's an outcast, just another person down on her luck. She's sick, she's run out of money, her life is in a shambles, and it's been going on for so long she can hardly remember what it's like to be a normal person. Jesus can't let her walk away without a word. It's not enough to rid her of her medical problem. That's just for starters.

"Daughter. . . your faith has done this. Go in peace and be healed." In other words: you trusted in God so much that you came down here and didn't let the crowd intimidate you. You worked your way past all the people and actually reached out and touched me. Your faith in God convinced you that you could do it and that you would be healed. You were right. I'm so proud of you! *Now...* trust God to help you with the rest of it. Start fresh. Renew your ties with other people. Get your life back together again. "Go in peace. . . and *be healed.*"

Meanwhile, Jairus is having fits. He's a religious leader himself so he understands how important all this is. It isn't enough for Jesus just to stop the woman's flow of blood. He has to take the additional steps to welcome her back into the community and to pronounce God's blessing upon her. Jairus realizes the significance of this moment. But his own daughter is dying and all he wants now is for Jesus to get there in time to save her. *Can't we move things along here?*

His worst fears are confirmed when he sees some of his friends approaching. They don't know how to tell him. "Jairus. . . dear Jairus. . . there's no need for you to trouble the Teacher any longer. Do you understand? There's no point anymore. . ."

His heart sinks. "Is she. . ?"

They nod.

So that's it, then. Gone! His only child—his one joy in life— gone! He turns his perplexed face toward Jesus. *He* could've saved her. He was on his way to do so.

*If it hadn't been for the crowd. If it hadn't been for that woman. . .*

## *Living on God's Schedule*

We never see Jesus in a hurry, not even in this story. Those around him may be panicked, and they may cry out to him, "Don't you care that we're getting slammed over here?" (Mark 4:38, paraphrased). He does care, but he doesn't let people rush him. He's living on God's schedule. For him, everything happens right on time.

Of course, *his* idea of "on time" may not be ours. It usually isn't. We want things to come much sooner than they actually end up coming. But if it's right for them to happen then they do so when they're supposed to.

Another thing that's hard about living on God's schedule is the interruptions. People interrupt Jesus all the time but he doesn't get cranky. If things happen at their appropriate time then there's no such thing as an interruption. What we would call an interruption is just God bringing about the thing that's supposed to happen right now, even though it may come in the middle of something else we're trying to do.

In his book, *The Christ of the Mount*, E. Stanley Jones gives this description of Jesus: "He comported himself in duty as on a holiday." That's a proper British way of saying, "Christ was so happy doing his work, you'd have thought he was on vacation." No, he didn't wear polo shirts and khakis. But he was relaxed and unperturbed. No matter how urgent the situation, he didn't lose his composure. He was living on God's schedule. . .

"*Jairus*. . ."

The grieving father turns his face to the Master, but he can't see through his tears.

"Don't be afraid," Jesus says. "Only believe."

Believe *what?* His daughter is dead. What's left to hope for?

But Jesus doesn't wait around. This time *he* takes the lead, leaving Jairus and his friends to stumble after him. When they arrive at the house, they find that people from the neighborhood have already gathered to mourn the girl's passing. They aren't just weeping; they're howling. They're totally unglued. *It's too late! Too late!*

Christ dismisses everybody but Jairus and his wife and three of his disciples. He knows the girl's parents need privacy, even if it takes extra time for him to arrange it.

In the quiet room, Jairus now kneels before his daughter and prays feverishly. His wife joins him on the floor, looking hopefully between her husband and the Master, trying to figure out what's about to happen.

Jesus calmly takes the child's hand and holds it. "Little girl," he says, "arise."

Her eyes blink open and she sits up. Jairus stops his prayer in mid-sentence. His wife grabs his arm and gasps. Then both parents bury their faces in the girl's lap, crying noisily. She stares at Jesus, totally confused, but he smiles back at her. Placing his hands on both parents' shoulders, he says, "She'll need something to eat."

### *Customer Casualty on Aisle Three*

Don't get me wrong. We shouldn't take so much time with one customer that another one dies waiting. I'm just saying that the imitation of Christ is all about living on God's schedule. We do what we can and we rely on God to help us accomplish things in their proper time. That allows us to keep our nerves steady when we're faced with unexpected delays, equipment failures, and other variables beyond our control.

But even if we're committed to living on God's timetable, we still need to realize that we're in a fast-paced line of work. For our clients' sakes, we must move quickly.

I was once a member of a six-person Help Desk team that answered phone calls from our company's internal departments. We knew a lot about policies and procedures and we were especially good at problem solving. We thought of ourselves as an elite unit. We were justifiably proud of our achievements.

One day our supervisor asked us in a team meeting, "What is your Number One Job?"

We gave what we thought was the right answer: "To serve our customers." But she surprised us by saying, "No, that's not it." We tried several versions of the same idea and got the same response.

Finally she told us, "Your Number One Job is to answer the phones."

We were great at assisting those who were able to get through to us, but a high percentage of the people calling into our department were not getting through. We were good at what we

RON JOHNSON

did but we weren't fast. And when those two measurements were pitted against each other, "good" wasn't good enough.

Imagine a long line of patrons waiting to get into a store. Many of them get inside and are thrilled with the service they receive. Many others are forced to wait outside in the rain until they finally stomp away in disgust. Under such circumstances, can we consider ourselves good at what we do?

This problem is always on the mind of a CSR, whether we work in a call center or in a face-to-face setting. No matter how much we may want to give excellent service to our clients, we cannot do so at the expense of those who are waiting. We're forced constantly to strike a balance between quality and quantity, between "wowing the customer" and keeping the line moving.

The solution? First, we should strive to live on God's schedule. That insures that we will not only remain calm but also seek divine assistance in doing everything in its proper time. But having set that priority, we should also look for ways to work more efficiently, for everybody's sake.

I struggled with this issue for years. Due to a company merger, I left the Help Desk and joined a larger department that worked under very different conditions. In this new setting, timing became more important than ever before. My scores weren't as good as my team leaders wanted, and although we discussed the problem month after month, we couldn't solve it. Finally I was teamed up with a coworker who provided the key insight: I was very busy during each call, doing things that were no longer necessary. For

78

example, I was trying to write everything down on a log and keep up on my computer, all at the same time. The writing was slowing me down.

My coworker asked me, "Do you ever go back to those call logs?" I thought about it and realized that the answer was No. There had once been a time when we were required to keep those logs in case our managers had questions about a call we had taken, but procedures had changed. Nobody ever asked me for that information anymore because everything was now captured by on-screen call logs. Without even thinking about it, I had incorporated the new procedures into the old and had made twice as much work for myself.

On her advice, I put aside my notepad and began focusing exclusively on the computer. This not only made me faster but also took a lot of stress off me and gave me greater freedom to converse with my customers. Many other insights followed from this initial one. Most of them stemmed from the same basic principle: that I was trying to do some things I didn't need to do anymore.

As this story illustrates, it's possible on most days to keep the line moving. Lots of good CSRs do it. If we have high call times, or if customers routinely complain that the other line is faster, then we can probably find ways to work more efficiently without giving poor service. We may have to be willing to listen to our managers' and coworkers' ideas, however, in order to make that happen.

But if you work in a call center, then you know I've been skirting around the real issue. Call center CSRs are constantly pressured to decrease their Average Handling Time (AHT). This is not the same as merely working faster for the sake of the customer. This is about increasing our productivity for the sake of the company.

A coworker covers her mouthpiece and says, "I can't get this lady off my phone. She's killing my stats!" *This lady*, of course, has no idea that she's creating a problem, nor should any customer ever have to worry about such things. But it happens in call centers all the time. Clients can feel the pressure. They know that the CSR is trying to get them off the phone. They just don't know why. There's a lot more going on here than customers realize—more than most CSRs have probably considered.

### *Average Handling Time (AHT)*

Common sense would dictate that a CSR's goal for Average Handling Time ought to be the minimum number of minutes it takes us to serve customers well. We should give great service and do it as quickly as we can so that both the clients we're serving and those who are in line behind them won't have to wait long. But that's not what AHT is all about. Nobody in management does a calculation like that. Nobody lists all the components of a high-quality call and adds up the minimum amount of time it would take to hit all those components. That's not how management sets AHT goals. Let me show you how they actually do it.

Suppose you've started a business of your own, and on top of everything else you've decided to budget one hour per day for answering customer complaints. (This example may seem a little farfetched, but play along with me for a moment.) So you open the phone lines and sixty customers want to talk to you. You've got one hour—not a second more—and you don't want to turn anybody away. Do the math: how much time can you give to each customer? Obviously, one minute.

Please note that this answer has nothing to do with offering good service. It's simply a mathematical problem. If you have only one hour and there are sixty clients waiting to talk to you, you'll either have to turn some of them away or answer each of them, on average, in a minute or less.

Of course, you can't get the job done in that amount of time, so you hire someone to help you. Now you only have to take thirty calls. In the course of one hour, how much time can you devote to each customer? Two minutes. Unfortunately, you've also doubled your costs, and your new employee is doing nothing to help you raise revenues. You've still got the same amount of money coming in, but more is going out than before. And what do you get for it? One more minute per client.

Ready to hire a third person? Go for it. Suddenly you've tripled your costs, but it's worth it, right? Because now you only have to talk to twenty customers, and you can spend even more of your sixty minutes talking to each one of them. Twenty customers in sixty minutes. How much time does that give you? Three minutes per caller.

I haven't even mentioned how long it would actually take to

have an effective conversation with any one of these customers. The question is, "How can you answer sixty calls per hour without turning anybody away?" And if we're going to frame the question like that, then the answer is not subject either to opinion or emotion. It's simply a mathematical problem, based on available resources.

This is what CSRs don't seem to realize. Upper management doesn't set AHT goals by calculating how long it takes to serve each customer well. Management forecasts how many calls will come in at peak times. They divide that by the number of employees available to take those calls, and the result is our AHT goal. Our AHT goal is simply the amount of time the company has allotted to us, on average, to respond to each customer, based on their forecast of future call volume and on the number of employees available to take those calls.

We may think that management should hire more CSRs, but that's not for us to say. We don't have to pay the bills. Remember this: we CSRs don't raise money for the company. We're not "productive" in that sense. But it costs a lot of money to employ us, to equip us with phones and computers, to train us (and keep us up-to-date after that), to establish 800 numbers, to offer us benefits, and so on. We're not bringing money in, but a lot of money's going out. From management's point of view, it's not going to solve the problem to hire more CSRs. The solution is to get the existing CSRs to keep to the allotted time.

But here's the thing I want to emphasize: our AHT goal has

nothing to do with our clients. It's not about serving them better or even faster. It's not a customer-driven metric. True, if we meet the goal then we are indeed answering each call faster, which means each caller has a shorter wait, but we're also rushing each customer in turn. And our clients do feel the pressure.

Another problem with AHT is that the same goal applies to everybody in the department even though we all have very different styles. Forget the customer for a moment, just for the sake of argument. Each of us has a minimum average time that we could maintain if we were really trying to do so. Depending on what the call is about, some cases take longer than others, but each of us could probably maintain a minimum average if we wanted to do so (and didn't mind hurrying our clients through each call). The problem is that *your* minimum average would be different from *mine* because we each have different working styles.

Some CSRs are methodical, asking all their questions up front. Even among that subgroup, some formulate answers in their heads as they go along while others suspend judgment until they've heard everything. In contrast, there are CSRs who are ready with an answer immediately, without asking a lot of questions. Others are extremely personable, making casual conversation with the client all along the way, artfully weaving questions in between pleasantries. Still others are born-educators, patiently explaining everything to customers in hopes of preventing misunderstandings in the future.

None of these styles are right or wrong. They merely reflect the differences in our personalities and thought processes. We approach each client interaction in ways that express who we are, and there's nothing wrong with that.

Unfortunately, when we have a single AHT goal for everyone in the department, that goal favors individuals whose styles are faster than those of their peers. Some CSRs are treated as superior performers simply because they have working styles that are quick. Even worse, the people with inherently slower styles are treated as poor performers and are pressured by their managers to do better. And we all buy into that assessment—we congratulate the winners and feel like we're bad CSRs if we don't meet the goal. We're missing the truth here. The truth is that the goal has nothing to do with giving good service. It's simply the amount of time that the company has allotted for each caller, based on the costs involved.

This, then, is the biggest timing problem that we'll face if we want to imitate Christ through customer service. *Our* main priority is to help others, but *upper management's* main priority is productivity. Given X number of projected callers and Y number of CSRs to answer the phones, management calculates that we must finish each call within a certain specified number of minutes, without taking into account whether we're capable of giving excellent service within that span of time. And there's the conflict. We may work quickly, but that doesn't mean we'll be able to abide by management's calculations. Living on God's schedule can be dangerous. If we're committed to serving others as Jesus would serve them, we might not achieve the goal that management has set for us. And therefore we might end up unemployed.

But AHT is only one aspect of a larger problem—the evaluation process—and for many CSRs, that process is the most difficult part of the job. I'll talk about that in the next chapter.

### Questions for Reflection and Discussion

1. Do your managers measure how long it takes you to serve each customer? Do you feel pressured by that fact? What can you do about it? Do you understand why speed is important in our line of work?

2. I showed you how our AHT goals are calculated. We certainly ought to understand why our managers want us— in fact, *need* us—to answer all the incoming calls. But if we can see that, how can we justify not meeting our department's goal?

3. What would it mean to live each day on God's schedule? What difference would it make in our personal lives if we did this? How would it affect our productivity as CSRs?

4. Do you think it's possible to be a CSR and still behave as if we're on vacation? How? Would you like to live like that? What's stopping you?

# 9 ALL FOR A JOLLY RANCHER®

The evaluation process is perhaps the hardest part of being a CSR. It casts a shadow over every customer interaction and influences most of our decisions. *Will I get marked down if I say such-and-such?* we ask ourselves. It's a valid question, because our every move is recorded and critiqued. It's not just annoying; it's hard on the soul.

This is another area in which the imitation of Christ can guide us, for it offers an alternative approach that will help us survive and possibly thrive under the rigorous evaluation process to which we're subjected each day.

## Life in the Fish Bowl

There are at least five reasons why CSR evaluations are hard on the soul.

First, every detail of our work is closely observed. Everything we do is monitored and documented. Our supervisors know

CUSTOMER SERVICE AND THE IMITATION OF CHRIST

exactly how long it takes us to service each customer and they have the whole thing on tape. Thanks to "screen capture," they see every move we make on the computer, every keystroke, and every click of the mouse. They even know when we go to the restroom and how long we're gone. Our life is an open book.

This is hard on the soul because we have no privacy, and at least a small degree of privacy is necessary for our well-being. It can also be difficult to have a Three-Way under these circumstances. On more than one occasion I've put my customer on hold and had an animated discussion with God about what to do next. When I started out as a CSR years ago, managers listened to our calls live and watched us from across the room. Imagine how perplexed they must have been if they heard me put the customer on hold and then watched and listened while I had a conversation with nobody! But the main problem is that we're tethered to our phones and closely monitored all day. That's not a good way for humans to conduct their lives, especially if we stay in a frontline position for many years.

Second, we aren't just watched—our words and actions are criticized. Anything we say or do is fair game. I once had a manager correct my grammar. I said "toward" and she thought it should be "towards." The fact that I had a PhD and she had just graduated from college didn't intimidate her. As my manager, she felt she had the authority to correct me. On another occasion, a coworker of mine was given a low score for saying "policy and procedures." She was told that they should both be plural (policies and procedures) and that her failure to use proper grammar reflected badly on the company.

Those are extreme examples, but we all know how wide a net our managers cast when critiquing us. They evaluate. . .

. . . Our vocal inflections. ("Get a smile in your voice," they tell us.)

. . . Our word choice. (We should never say, "I don't know," even if we truly don't know. We should say, "Let me check on that." We'll be marked down if we say in a friendly voice, "I don't know but let me check on that." An honest admission of ignorance is considered unprofessional.)

. . . Our quoting of the script. (It's not enough to help our customers. First we have to say, "I'll be *glad* to help you." If we forget to say it then we'll receive a low score no matter how effectively we solve the customer's problem.)

. . . Our use of the client's name at least twice.

. . . How well we manage the call. (It's up to us to maintain control of the conversation at all times and to keep it moving toward quick resolution. This includes AHT, which I already talked about in the previous chapter, but there's much more to it than that. We deal with a wide range of personalities and we're expected to keep control of the call no matter how vigorously our customers may try to take the lead.)

. . . How closely we comply with our assigned schedule. (If we're supposed to go on lunch at 12:45 but we're stuck on a call until 12:55, we're out of compliance. We have to finish servicing the customer, but it lowers our score if we don't return from lunch at the assigned time.)

. . . How often we ask for help. (If we need help and don't request it, we'll be marked down, but it counts against us every time we ask.)

And so on. It's like a chess game. Everything we do or fail to do can come back to bite us. We have to work quickly but we also have to think carefully about everything that comes out of our mouths. And if we allow a moment of silence to occur while we stop to weigh our words, we'll have points deducted for "dead air."

A lot depends on how our managers approach the evaluation process. Some team leaders celebrate our strengths and offer useful strategies for improving our scores. Others treat us like children. I once had a supervisor play one of my recorded calls during a team meeting in order to point out what *not* to do. I wanted to sink down in my chair and crawl out of the room.

But upper management sets the mood by the terms they use. I've worked for companies that call these evaluation sessions "coaching" (which has a nice, jaunty tone to it) while others refer to them as "counseling"—like there's something wrong with us. Some companies call CSRs "unproductive" if they don't meet the department's AHT goal. Oh, the power of words! A CSR may lead the department in giving excellent service and still be treated like a freeloader if she doesn't work quickly enough. As I said in the previous chapter, customer service is not revenue-producing so *no* CSR is truly productive. For that matter, neither is anyone in upper management. But the people in those top seats decide what criteria they'll accept *in place of* productivity and then they think of just the right words to shame us if we don't comply.

But even when our managers take our feelings into account and our company is sensitive to its use of language, the evaluation process itself is still hard on the soul. We CSRs are critiqued in much greater detail than we would be in almost any other line of work. Everything we say and do is subject to criticism all day long. At best, we need thick skins. At worst, humiliation awaits.

### *Dogs and Dolphins*

The third reason the evaluation process is so hard is that our company is deliberately trying to reshape our behavior. They aren't monitoring us for the fun of it. They point out our shortcomings because they expect us to change. There's a name for what they're doing: it's called *behavior modification*. It's what animal trainers use in teaching dogs or dolphins to perform tricks. When the animals exhibit proper behavior they're rewarded and when they don't they're corrected. Our managers correct us so that we'll speak and act the way the people in the corporate office want us to speak and act. That's the point of the whole evaluation process.

Don't get me wrong. I'm not blaming management for trying to shape our behavior. It's not their fault. This is just the way the role of a CSR has evolved, and we can understand why it's done this way. But it's still hard on our souls. Why? Because the intent is to compel us to speak and act according to someone else's dictates. We knew all about this when we were hired so it's not like our supervisors are being devious. We're consenting adults. But that doesn't make it any better. In return for a paycheck, it feels like we're selling our souls. We're letting them "correct" and "counsel" us and change our behavior. And we can't agree to something like that without feeling the results deep in our hearts.

It may seem overly dramatic for me to say "it feels like we're selling our souls," but here's what I mean by that. Each of us was born with our own unique personality which over the years has evolved into our own patterns of thought, our own style of problem-solving, our facial expressions, voice inflection, conversation skills, and so on. *That's who we are.* Hopefully we'll continue to grow and improve throughout our lives, and the demands of our job may exert a certain amount of influence on some of those improvements. But in a healthy situation, we're deliberate about such changes—*we* decide whether we're going to adjust our way of speaking or revise our thought patterns, and *if* we choose to do so, then *we* determine what changes we'll make.

That's what happens in a healthy work environment. But when we became CSRs, we agreed to let our employer tell us how and when we will smile, how to conduct a conversation, how to solve problems, and so on. We didn't just sell them our time or our labor—we sold them the right to make adjustments in our personality. We can be whoever we want to be when our shift is over, but during working hours we must think, speak, and act according to their script. I know of no other job that places such demands on the total person. If that's not what it feels like to sell our souls, then I don't know what those words mean.

Some of you may lack firsthand experience of this. Perhaps your working style naturally coincides with upper management's ideal. Your scores are high, or at least high enough for you to be exempt from the reshaping process that your coworkers are laboring under. It's happening all around you but it doesn't affect you directly.

Or perhaps you're so passionate about customer service that you've been promoted to team leader, trainer, manual writer, or something like that. Your time on the frontlines may have been short, and during that period you were excited about your work and about the prospects for advancement. You made it through the evaluation process intact because you didn't feel its full effect. You gladly accepted feedback that would help you on your way to better things. You dodged the full force of the process.

But even if you yourself haven't borne the brunt of it, I hope you can see that that's what's happening. The point of the evaluation process is behavior modification, and if a CSR's behavior can't be modified to fit the ideal, then that person becomes subject to disciplinary action and is eventually fired or pressured to leave. And like I said, when we were hired we knew that that was what the job entailed, so we go along with it. But that doesn't mean it's healthy.

## *It's a Dog-Eat-Dog Job*

Here's the fourth reason that the evaluation process is hard on the soul: because it's highly competitive. Our scores are tabulated, we're stack-ranked against our peers, and the results are posted for all to see. The names of those who are lower in the ranking may be masked, but we all know where we stand relative to the people at the top, and that's the point. Our managers expect us to look at these scores daily and to make whatever corrections we can in order to improve.

We Americans have a high regard for competitive sports, but in the workplace it's bad for the soul. It may be fun to see who wins when two good teams are pitted against each other, but in the workplace that kind of mentality is inappropriate. Each one of us has an important job to do and there's no reason why anyone should lose. That metaphor simply doesn't belong in a work environment. Unfortunately, CSR evaluations are thoroughly competitive because management believes that peer pressure is a strong incentive. As with any competition, however, only a very few people can win. That makes the rest of us losers, at least to some extent.

Besides this, in my experience very few CSRs are spurred on by the desire to win or by a passion to become one of the top people. It's much more common to hear CSRs fret about *not* winning. "I'm stuck on this call and it's ruining my stats," they say. "I'll never make goal if this keeps up!" Or, "Did you see how badly I did yesterday? I'll never catch up now!" That kind of worrying is not good for anybody's soul, nor does it serve management's purpose. It just makes life more difficult for CSRs.

Finally, the evaluation process is hard on the soul because it undermines our own natural motivation by seeking to "incent" us. I once worked for managers who used exactly those terms: they talked frequently about what it would take to "incent" CSRs—in other words, to motivate us to do what they wanted us to do. Remember what I said at the beginning of this book? If we're in our right minds, most people want to be helpful. We're already strongly motivated to do so just by virtue of the fact that we're human. But upper management doesn't trust us to care about our customers. They devise an elaborate system of incentives and disincentives to make us want to do our jobs. And like I said a moment ago, if we're on the lower end of the stack ranking, then the punishments influence us much more strongly than do the rewards.

I once had a manager who was very good at shaming her employees when we disappointed her but not so skilled at rewarding us. She seemed to believe that she could motivate us with a small food item for good behavior. How do you get CSRs to improve their AHT, raise their quality scores, and reduce their escalations? Promise them a piece of hard candy. I was fairly new to customer service and I found that appalling. She not only expected us to sell our souls—she wanted us to sell them cheap. She thought she could buy them with a Jolly Rancher®!

As I said a moment ago, however, if we're already struggling then we'll be more strongly motivated by threats than by promises. Most of us are in this line of work because we need a paycheck and insurance, not because we chose to do this for a living. We can't afford to lose our job. That's what keeps us working hard. Candy and recognition are equally unimportant. We don't want to end up in the unemployment line. Short of that, however, we also don't want to be treated like buffoons. We do whatever we can to avoid being on the bottom of the stack ranking or to keep from being singled out as negative examples.

Why is this situation bad for the soul? Because as humans we naturally want to help others, but management replaces that natural desire with a system of artificial rewards and punishments, and the punishments hang over our heads, "incenting" us to do whatever is necessary to avoid humiliation and eventual termination. Instead of treating us like mature adults, this system casts us in the role of children.

I've been saying that the evaluation process is hard on *us*, but it's also not very friendly to our clients. The scoring process takes our focus off our customers and shapes our behavior in ways that are not conducive to giving good service. We're so intent on saying our customers' names, following the script, not escalating to a senior rep, completing the call quickly, and meeting our sales quota—not to mention starting our lunch on time—that our minds are only partly available for our customers. If they need something special from us, they may have to raise their voice to get our attention. And that's not good for anybody: the CSR, the client, or the company. But that's how it works in today's call centers.

You may be wondering, *How can the imitation of Christ provide a solution to a problem of this magnitude?* I believe it can, and I'll tell you how in the next chapter.

## *Questions for Reflection and Discussion*

1. Have you been "coached" or "counseled" for not meeting management objectives? How did it make you feel? Have you found ways to maintain your sense of dignity at such moments?

2. What kinds of prizes and incentives (or disincentives) do your managers offer? Do these things help motivate you? Please be specific about what works and doesn't work.

3. I said that the CSR evaluation process is aimed at modifying our behavior. Do you think that's a fair assessment? Why or why not?

4. If you do recognize that behavior modification is the purpose of the process, can you understand why I say it feels like we're selling our souls if we go along with it? Do you feel that way sometimes?

# 10 THE SELF-EXAMINED LIFE

In the previous chapter I talked about what's wrong with CSR evaluations. Now I'll tell you how the imitation of Christ can help us make the most of our coaching sessions. *Make the most of them?* you may ask. Yes! We don't want to circumvent the process. We want to use it to everyone's advantage. In the pages ahead I'll tell you how we can do that.

## *Our True Incentive*

First we've got to get our priorities straight, and we do that by taking a better look at the Person we're trying to imitate. As I said in chapter 2, Christ worked long hours and was strongly motivated to rise early and start each new day. What "incented" him? He tells us: "I must work the works of him who sent me while it is day; night is coming when no one can work" (John 9:4). He was determined to bring about his Father's will on earth, and he was aware of the urgency of his mission. According to the prevalent belief, God's work was finished on the seventh day of creation, but Christ denied that. "My Father is still working," he insisted, "and I also am working" (John 5:17).

He tried to pass on that work ethic to his disciples: "Very truly, I tell you, the one who believes in me will also do the works that I do and, in fact, will do greater works than these, because I am going to the Father" (John 14:12). Let's not get bogged down speculating on precisely how our work today can be considered greater than the works he did in his day. The important thing here is that he's depending on us to continue his Father's work. "As the Father has sent me, so I send you" (John 20:21).

He doesn't mean "if you have time" or "for a few hours after your shift is over." He's calling us to do his Father's work all the time, everywhere. That's our top priority if we're committed to the imitation of Christ.

He says we have to make a choice, and it goes to the root of the problem I've been talking about: "No servant can serve two masters, for either he will hate the one and love the other, or he will be devoted to the one and despise the other. You cannot serve God and mammon" (Luke 16:13, RSV). "Mammon" is the New Testament word for "wealth" or "riches."

You may laugh at this because nobody ever got rich being a CSR. But he's trying to show us that the thing we're focused on will determine everything else. "For where your treasure is, there your heart will be also" (Matthew 6:21). And if we're doing this job primarily for the paycheck, small though it may be, then we're in the service of mammon.

He drives this point home with a story (Luke 16:1-12). A rich man realizes that one of his employees has been feathering his own nest using company funds. He confronts the employee and fires him. But the employee seizes the moment. Before word gets out that he's been fired, he visits all the people who owe his company money.

"How much did we charge you?" he asks the first debtor.

"One hundred dollars," is the reply.

"Let's make it fifty and call it good," he says. Thrilled at these words, the debtor writes him a check.

"How much do you owe?" he asks the next debtor.

Again the answer is, "One hundred dollars."

"Give me eighty now and we'll forget the whole thing," he says.

"Great!" And the debtor pays him.

What happens next isn't clear. It looks like the dishonest steward pockets the money and runs. But that doesn't make sense because the text says that his objective is to make friends with all the debtors so that they'll take him in when he's poor. And of course they won't do that when they find out that he ran off with their money and they still owe his employer the same amount as before.

It could be that he returns to his employer and says, "Look, none of these people were going to pay you back but I got them to sit down and write you a check for most of what they owed. Will you accept that?" Then the employer's happy because he recouped losses he thought he'd have to write off. And the debtors are happy because they didn't have to pay the full amount. So the guy comes out ahead. He gets his job back and the debtors think he's a hero.

The text doesn't say how the story ends, but the guy comes out ahead somehow. And Jesus' commentary is startling: "I tell you, make friends for yourselves by means of unrighteous mammon, so that when it fails they may receive you into eternal habitations" (v. 9, RSV). In plain English: "Use whatever money, status, or power you have to get ahead now. That way, if you ever get into financial trouble down the line, people will help you because they'll owe you favors. You'll even get into heaven that way!"

What a strange thing to say! It isn't just *foreign* to Christian faith; it's *opposed* to it. Christ seems to be telling us to rely on material wealth and social status to get ahead in the world—and even in the next world.

But here's what I think he's saying. Sometimes we're tempted to play the game like everybody else, to do whatever's necessary to get ahead. But if we're going to do it at all, why not go all the way? Why do it half-heartedly? The people who are really good at lying, cheating, and stealing win the admiration of their society. Frank Abignale's book, *Catch Me If You Can*, became a bestseller and Steven Spielberg even made a movie about it. If you're going to bend the rules, bend them in a big way, then you'll become a hero. Everyone will admire you. Who knows? Maybe you'll even be able to cheat your way into heaven. After all, if everyone admires you, maybe the priest will too, and he'll give you absolution.

But. . .

If you want to follow Christ's way, you'll need to obey it even in the little things. No straying from the path now and then, just to get ahead. "Whoever is faithful in a very little is faithful also in much," Christ goes on to say; "and whoever is dishonest in a very little is dishonest also in much" (v. 10). If we allow ourselves to do it the world's way even occasionally, even for the sake of a small paycheck, then we're not faithful followers of Christ and his way. We're simply mediocre followers of the way of the world—not really successful at getting ahead but still following that way of life, more or less.

You may ask, "But what about my paycheck? I've got to feed my family."

Jesus realizes that, but he wants us to recognize what's most important: ". . . and indeed your heavenly Father knows that you need all these things. But strive first for the kingdom of God and his righteousness, and all these things will be given to you as well" (Matthew 6:32-33).

First things first, then! As we go about our jobs as CSRs, are we going to do it as imitators of Christ or are we going to worry about our score? That's the crucial question. I'm not saying that our score is totally unimportant. I'm just saying we have to decide what's *most* important. For whether we want to admit it or not, the evaluation process asks us to rent out our total personalities, which (as I said earlier) makes us feel like we're selling our souls. "For what shall it profit a man, if he shall gain the whole world, and lose his own soul?" (Mark 8:36 KJV). We're not trying to "gain the whole world." We're just trying to put food on the table. But in exchange for that small favor we're giving our employer free reign in critiquing our personalities. Christ is reminding us that it's not worth it.

Bottom line? We can't afford to let management "incent" us. If we want to be CSRs who imitate Christ, then our primary motivation should be to do Christ's work rather than to get a good score. That's our starting point.

## Who Loves You, Baby?

If our goal is to imitate Christ, then we want essentially the same thing management does: we want to serve our customers well. Upper management wants it for economic reasons (to grow the company) and we want it for personal reasons (because we care about people and want to be like Jesus). Although we have different motives, we aim for the same thing. And in order to accomplish that, we will need to evaluate ourselves daily. Here's how *our* evaluation process works.

It begins with an extremely positive fact: that we're in the service of someone who loves us and wants the very best for us. We aren't just imitating Christ in the way that philosophers imitate Socrates. We have a personal relationship with Jesus through the Holy Spirit. The Spirit knows us and cares about us.

And it goes even deeper: "But God proves his love for us in that while we still were sinners Christ died for us" (Romans 5:8). He initiated the relationship and paid the ultimate price to make it possible. And he did it "while we still were sinners." We didn't earn his love and we couldn't do so even if we tried. By the same token, nothing can separate us from God's love (Romans 8:31-39). What a great way to start an evaluation!

But then we get serious, because God doesn't just love *us*— God loves everyone, and Christ is enlisting us in his service precisely to help share God's love with others. Because God first loved us, we're strongly motivated to pass on that love to others in Jesus' name. But in many respects we're not like Jesus. No matter how nice we may be, we're not as kind and loving as he is. We're striving to *become* like him and we hope to reach that goal someday, but we're not there yet. And especially since we CSRs work under a lot of constraints (as I've outlined throughout this book), we know how hard it is for us to be like him under these trying circumstances. So we're constantly measuring ourselves against Christ and doing what we can to become more like him on the job.

What's important here is that we're personally committed to our own self-examination. It's not about getting better scores. It's about becoming more like Jesus. That's our ultimate goal and nobody wants that for us more than we do. We don't have to be offered incentives. All on our own, we want to become faster and more competent so that we can serve our customers like Christ would if he were here in the flesh.

This is crucial. If we're determined to examine ourselves and take responsibility for our own self-improvement, then we're not selling our souls. If we make any changes in the way we speak or act, we do it voluntarily. We're not being shaped passively by behavior modification. We're working together with God to become more like Jesus. That makes all the difference.

But as I just said, we're working together with God by means of the Holy Spirit. In practical terms, that happens as we practice a lively Three-Way CSR Conversation, because a Three-Way has evaluation built into it. A Three-Way, after all, is a spot-check prayer vigil. We're listening for what God is saying to us as events play out. We don't wait until we're tired in the evening and ask God, "How did I do today?" We touch base throughout the day, moment-by-moment. And if we're doing it right, then it's an ongoing process of self-evaluation in God's presence.

Here's an example of how it works when we're not on the job. We're driving down the highway and someone cuts us off. We honk our horn.

"Hmm," says the inner voice, "would Jesus do that?"

Or we see a person in need and we turn away thinking, *Aw, that's too bad.*

"Really?" says the inner voice. "Are you sure you can't do something about it?"

We're listening to our conscience in these Three Ways—a conscience informed by the teachings of Jesus. But the Spirit inspires our thinking and gives us insights that will help us recognize what God wants us to do.

In earlier chapters I gave examples of how this works on the job: how the Spirit reminds us not to judge our customers (chapter 5) and guides us as we try to resolve difficult problems (chapter 7). We're working together with God and critiquing ourselves *while* we're working. For two thousand years, Christians have engaged in self-examination during moments of prayer and meditation, but in a Three-Way CSR Conversation we do it *while we're taking calls*. Of course, we should also set aside time to pray and evaluate ourselves when we're not busy trying to serve others. But the beauty of the Three-Way CSR Conversation is that we check in with God throughout our day, striving to let the Spirit work through us.

### Welcoming Feedback

We can't be satisfied with our own self-evaluation, though. If we want to know how our clients perceive us then we need to get other perspectives. In our personal life, for example, family and friends sometimes have to point out things we do that we didn't realize we were doing, like whistling through our nose or talking too loud. Of course, just because our friends or loved ones tell us their perceptions, that doesn't mean we have to change, but if we care about them then we'll want to do what we can to improve our relationships with them.

It's the same thing in our jobs. We need others to tell us how we're doing. As CSRs, we're fortunate to have a lot of objective data that people in other lines of work don't have. In the previous chapter I noted that our calls are recorded, and now that turns out to be a boon for us because it provides us with valuable information. Some CSRs cringe at hearing their own voice on tape, but we need to hear ourselves as we actually sound to the customer. If we come across as though we're bored, rude, or in a hurry, we want to know about that so we can correct it. By playing back our calls, we can learn whether we're listening carefully to our clients, whether they seem to understand what we're telling them, and many other things that may escape our notice when we're actively involved in a call.

We also have other kinds of objective data: our stats. In the last chapter I talked about how those numbers make our lives miserable if we allow them to do so, but in this context we recognize how useful they can be. The key here is that we are in charge of our own self-examination. As long as we remember that, we should never fear to look at our AHT, our escalations, and all those other numbers that make up our total score. We aren't "incented" by our score, but we do care very much about how well we're serving our customers, and those numbers provide us with important information.

Even if our department's AHT score is unrealistic (as I argued in chapter 8 that it may indeed be), we should still want to know how long it's taking us to serve our clients and we should look for ways to serve them faster. If we frequently call our senior reps for help, it may indicate that we're not as knowledgeable as we should be. Although it hurts, we need to know the facts about ourselves and weigh them carefully, for as Christ says, "the truth will make you free" (John 8:32). This is a crucial part of our self-evaluation. It tells us what we need to do to improve in our imitation of Christ.

Perhaps it sounds like I'm contradicting myself. Are we supposed to obsess about our stats after all? The answer is No. Our goal is to be like Jesus, and that means we want to serve people as well as he would if he were here in our place. That's an ambitious goal and we'll spend the rest of our lives trying to reach it. But in order to direct our efforts, we want to know if we're working too slowly, if we ask for help too frequently, if our voice tone puts people off, and so on. That doesn't mean we should sigh and moan every time we see our stats go up. It just means we should turn to God in our Three-Way and think carefully about our performance. If we know we can do better, we should simply confess that. The point isn't to get upset when we fail to meet the department's goals; it's to get an accurate picture of how well we're meeting our customers' needs. Even if we don't interpret the numbers the same way management does, we should always welcome statistical measurements. We want all the objective data we can get, because that'll help us chart our course.

"Yes," you may reply, "but what about our supervisors? Self-evaluation is fine, but we still have to meet with our team leaders and listen to their appraisal of us. That's the hard part." I agree that it *can* be. But it can also be an invigorating experience. It depends in large part on what you and I bring to those sessions.

The typical team leader was once a frontline CSR who was promoted because she demonstrated extraordinary enthusiasm and leadership ability. In most cases our supervisors care about our customers as much as, or more than, we do. As we travel up the line of authority, we'll still find managers who share our concern for giving great service, but they may not know what it's like on the frontlines. Most team leaders do. They've been there.

In other words, we now have an opportunity to sit down with someone who has survived and thrived as a CSR, and to hear their ideas about how we can improve. If we really want to do better, then we'll welcome their comments and our willingness to change will show. If some team leaders insist on scolding us, there's nothing we can do but grin and bear it. At such times, we have to remember whose we are. I try to carry on a Three-Way during these sessions, so the Spirit can guide me. But I've found that most team leaders want to be helpful, and when we convey our determination to improve, they're eager to offer suggestions without insulting us.

Of course, there's plenty of room for conflict in the things I've been saying. After all, I've been advising you not to fret if you don't meet your department's goals, because those goals don't take into account your individual working style or the needs of your customers. Although it sounds like I'm advocating rebellion, that's not my intention. Let me put it another way. Above all, we should be committed to serving people in Jesus' name. We can't use that as an excuse for working slowly or being incompetent. If we're totally serious about serving others in Jesus' name then we'll constantly find ways to improve and we'll welcome our team leaders' suggestions. But if, in the presence of God, we honestly believe that we're doing (roughly) the best we can do, then we're not obligated to hang our heads in shame just because our managers expect us to do even better. I don't recommend that we argue with them. We should just know in our hearts that their goals are different from ours.

Remember this, however: if we're committed to serving others in Jesus' name, that includes our managers. We're here to minister to them, too. And if they're pressuring us to improve, it's because *their* managers are pressuring *them*. We should do whatever we can to help them as long as it doesn't prevent us from serving our customers.

Some of my team leaders have stuck their necks out for me, and it has pained me to see them do it. I'm willing to pay the price of my commitment to Christ even if it comes to disciplinary action. But over the years, some of my supervisors have resisted disciplining me even when they were supposed to do so. That's why I've tried very hard to reach departmental goals despite the fact that I've disagreed with those goals philosophically: because I didn't want to let my team leaders down. We must always remember that our managers are people and we're called to serve them, too. And as I said a moment ago, I have a lot of respect for most of the managers I've known. They're as committed to quality as I am. But it's their job to get us to meet the goals that have been set by their superiors. Even if we disagree about those goals, we should do whatever we can to help our managers.

## No Contest

In the previous chapter I pointed out what's wrong with the typical CSR evaluation process, and in this chapter I've been telling you how the imitation of Christ can help us overcome those problems. Here's something else: in the previous chapter I said that the competitive nature of CSR evaluations can harm our souls. However, when we're committed to the imitation of Christ, we don't have that problem. There's no contest. We want everyone to win. We root for our coworkers and celebrate their successes. Nor do we consider ourselves deficient if we don't have as high a score as others do. We recognize each person as unique.

Christ illustrates this point during his last recorded conversation with Simon Peter. Peter has just learned some bad news about his future (John 21:15-19). Glancing over at the Apostle John, he asks, "Lord, what about him?" (v. 21). Peter seems to be saying, "I've always suspected that John was your favorite. Is his future going to be as grim as mine?"

Jesus tells him: "If it is my will that he remain until I come, what is that to you? Follow me!" (v. 22). In other words, "It won't do you any good to compare yourself to the other guy. What if he does have a rosy future? How does that help you deal with your situation? Forget about him. Follow me." This is worded more strongly in the Greek text than in the English translation because of the way the subject is emphasized. In the Greek he says, "*You* follow me." He seems to be saying, "Don't *you* worry about what I'm going to ask *him* to do. *You* must follow the path that's set before *you*."

That's why we CSRs shouldn't get caught up in the competitive nature of the evaluation process. If we're imitating Christ then we must focus on the path that's set before *us*. Others may be treated like superstars because they consistently meet departmental goals, but that should not concern us. We've got to follow the path set before *us*.

The imitation of Christ also prevents us from seeking awards. If they're offered to us, we shouldn't be nasty about it. We should accept kudos graciously, appreciating the fact that our managers value our efforts. But we must always keep clear in our minds why we're doing what we do, and who it is we're working for. As his followers, we should neither seek prizes nor fear reprisals. We aren't "incented" that way.

That was Jesus' complaint about the religious leaders of his era—that they were motivated by the desire for praise and special honors and not by the desire to help those in need (Matthew 23:5-7; Mark 12:38-39; Luke 20:46). The exaltation we want is from God, not from humans. And don't get me wrong: we do want to feel good about our performance. But it all comes down to what God thinks. We want to know whether God considers us "good and faithful servants" (Matthew 25:21 KJV). *That's* the focus of *our* evaluation process.

And finally, we should celebrate any time we're aware that God has ministered to someone through us. That's how we get our kicks if we're committed to the imitation of Christ. We'll be on the lookout for people we can help and bless, and whenever we get an opportunity to do any of those things, it's party time. Remember the Parable of the Prodigal Son (Luke 15:11-32)? The guy's life has gone to the dogs, but he turns it around. And what does his dad do? He throws a party.

Christ says it's like a lady who lives hand-to-mouth and she loses her paycheck (Luke 15:1-2, 8-10). (In the parable, it's a coin, but it's worth a day's wages.) She turns the house inside out looking for it. When she finds it, she dances a little jig and hurries to the back fence to share the good news with her neighbors. That's a metaphor for the imitation of Christ. We're looking for lost ones and celebrating when they're found.

Let me clarify something. All this talk about saving the lost makes it sound like we're supposed to proselytize. And yes, Christ does say that we're responsible for telling people about him (Matthew 10:32; Luke 12:8-9). But he's depending on us to do much more than that. He's trying to redeem the world in every possible way, and he's inviting us to be part of that. This is a comprehensive vision, and it includes any kind of good we can do—even something as simple as sharing a cup of cold water (Matthew 10:42). So don't let all this talk about saving the lost distract you. We're not just Bible thumping here. We're talking about being God's agents of peace in a turbulent world, and you and I have opportunities to do that every day in this job.

But don't miss the most important part: it's supposed to be fun. Celebration should be a way of life for us. Flip through the teachings of Jesus and you'll be surprised how often he compares the Kingdom of God to a party of some sort—a dinner, a wedding, or even a dance. It's not supposed to be drudgery. There's nothing more thrilling than working with Jesus. And that's why we're highly motivated to do it well.

So... how do we keep from selling our souls in this job? Through the imitation of Christ. If we want to serve others as Christ did, then we'll constantly evaluate ourselves and strive to improve. No one will shape our behavior externally. We'll listen eagerly to criticism and suggestions from our managers but we'll choose for ourselves how we'll respond. Nor will we worry about where we stand in the rankings. We'll wish all of our coworkers well and try to do our own personal best. If we're threatened with disciplinary action, we'll do what we can to improve but we won't get distracted from our main objective: to serve others in Jesus' name.

You may ask, "But what if we lose our jobs?" In extreme situations, that might happen—I'm not going to whitewash that. But it won't do us any good to live in fear. It may be that we're called to serve someplace else. We'll have to trust God to guide us. But the question is, Are we serious about imitating Christ even if it costs us our jobs? If we are, then he promises to be with us, helping us by means of his Spirit. In this book I've described the many ways in which that help comes. But there's one more benefit that I want to talk about, and I'll tell you about that in the closing chapter.

## *Questions for Reflection and Discussion*

1. Do you understand why it's so important for CSRs to choose between God and mammon, even if we don't earn much money? Have you made a conscious choice?

2. Are you able to accept criticism from your team leader without taking it personally? How do you maintain your sense of self-esteem? Does it help to realize that you're working for Someone who loves you no matter how much you may need to improve?

3. Can you applaud the successes of your coworkers without feeling bad about your own shortcomings? How do you stay focused on doing your own personal best?

4. As a CSR, have you helped Christ "save the lost" in any concrete ways lately? I'm not asking you to brag. I'm asking if you're able to identify ways in which you've allowed Christ to minister to others through you as a CSR. And here's the main question: if Christ *has* ministered to others through you, have you taken time to celebrate?

# 11 THE QUEST FOR REST

Raise your hand if you're tired. (Or just moan softly.)

Customer service work takes a heavy toll on people. A CSR in a call center once complained to her husband about it, and he was unsympathetic. "How can you be exhausted?" he asked. "You sit on your hind quarters all day!" (Those weren't his exact words, but this is a religious book.) He didn't recognize the wear-and-tear that's involved in this line of business.

I've been telling you about the spiritual benefits of imitating Christ through customer service. Here's another one.

## The Promise of Rest

Jesus says, "Come to me, all you that are weary and carrying heavy burdens, and I will give you rest. Take my yoke upon you, and learn from me; for I am gentle and humble in heart, and you will find rest for your souls. For my yoke is easy, and my burden is light" (Matthew 11:28-30).

Let's take this a phrase at a time:

*". . . all you that are weary and carrying heavy burdens. . ."*

We certainly qualify. Lots of other people do too, of course, and we must never forget that. This world is full of weary people. Many of them are our customers. But right now I'm talking about CSRs.

*"Come to me. . . and I will give you rest."*

Some extra vacation time would be nice, but that's not what he's talking about. He's offering us something we can use on the job: a new orientation toward life and work—a powerful inner dynamic that will make us become like him. And since *he* lived like he was *always* on vacation, that's supposed to rub off on us, too.

*"Take my yoke upon you. . ."*

A yoke is what an ox wears so that it can do hard labor. Yoked oxen trudge around and around the grindstone. Or they plod along in a field dragging a tiller behind them, digging furrows into the ground. "Putting on the yoke" is a metaphor conjuring up hard physical labor like a beast of burden. The thing is, we're already wearing a yoke—that's why we're so tired. We're yoked to our company. And we can't just throw off the yoke, because we have bills to pay. Christ doesn't want us to do that, anyway. He invites us to replace that hateful yoke with another one. He wants us to join *his* workforce and be in *his* service. It's the same job but we're under new management. Same customers, different focus.

*". . . and learn from me. . ."*

This means not only to become intimately acquainted with his teachings but also to practice them and become adept at doing them. We've talked about a few of them in this book. Notice that he says "learn *from* me." We aren't just learning *about* him. He himself is teaching us through the Holy Spirit as we practice Three-Way communication with him in everything we do.

*". . . for I am gentle and humble in heart. . ."*

He's no slave-driver. He loves us. He wants the best for us. But he knows that what's best for us is to do what we're really good at, and to use those skills to help others.

*". . . and you will find rest for your souls."*

Like I said, he's not going to take us off the frontlines. The rest he offers comes from within. It happens as we practice imitating him and following his teachings.

It's the surge of energy we experience when we join him in saying, "I want to help!" (Chapter 2).

It's the thrill we feel when we set out to do the seemingly-impossible (Chapter 3).

It's the rush we get from plugging into the Ultimate Power Source (Chapter 4).

It's the burden of negativity lifted off our shoulders when we stop judging our customers and learn to empathize (Chapter 5).

It's the great upswelling inside us when we become committed to blessing others—even those who are cursing us (Chapter 6).

It's the exhilaration that comes when we realize we're not alone but are part of a network of people who care (Chapter 7).

It's the inner strength and increased efficiency that come from living on God's schedule (Chapter 8).

It's the resolve we get when we stop worrying about our score and we take responsibility for our own self-evaluation (Chapters 9-10).

It's all of these things and more, because it's a gift renewed daily in a multitude of ways—a gift from the One whose yoke we share.

*"For my yoke is easy, and my burden is light."*

Let's be clear about this. What he's asking us to do isn't easy. When he says, "My burden is light," he means that we don't have to shoulder the burden alone. He offers us a buoyancy of the spirit that comes from yoking ourselves to him and harnessing *his* energy. *He* ends up ministering to needy people *through* us. Instead of sapping our strength, it energizes us.

Granted, there are days when we go home dog tired. That just means we're still learning how to redistribute the load so that it doesn't fall so heavily on us. It's a process. But we're working on it! It's just important for us to realize it isn't a vacation that we need—it's a new life. And that's Christ's specialty.

### CSR for the Rest of Your Life?

My last remark may have made you angry. Perhaps you're wondering, "What if I'm stuck being a CSR for the rest of my life? What kind of new life will Christ offer me then?" The answer is: a life of acceptance and adventure as you and God work through it together, one day at a time. That's been my experience.

I left a management position in customer service to earn my doctorate in philosophy, and for a few years after graduate school I was fortunate enough to teach full time. But I was only filling in for professors who were away on sabbatical, and when they returned home I was unable to obtain an academic appointment for the coming school year. I started searching for a day job. For weeks I was unsuccessful because employers felt I was overqualified, not only because I had a PhD but also because I had been a manager. Nobody wanted to take a chance on hiring me for an entry-level position. They thought I wouldn't be happy and would quit.

Finally I walked into an open house for call center CSRs and leveled with the interviewer. "I can give you one year," I told her, "and then I hope to be teaching again next fall." She admitted that the turnover rate for call centers is pretty high, and many CSRs don't even stick around for a year. So she was willing to give me a try.

That was eleven years ago, and at this writing I'm still working in the call center. My company has been bought out twice and my job duties have significantly changed, but I'm still taking phone calls all day. I do teach college courses at night and online, and I use my gifts and education through seminars, speaking engagements, and writing. But the call center is still my day job.

Of course, I can't predict what will happen to you. Maybe you won't be a CSR for the remainder of your life. This may just be a stop along the way for you. That's between you and God. But this much I can tell you: that even if you go on to do something else, the time you spend imitating Christ now as a CSR can prepare you to be service-minded in anything else you do in the years ahead. I'm not saying that customer service work itself will necessarily do that for you. I'm saying that, if you accept the invitation to *imitate Christ* as a CSR now, then you will learn lessons that will stay with you for the rest of your life.

And the world certainly needs service-oriented people, at all levels and all places of employment. Let me give you just a few examples.

(1) An elderly woman sees a guy from the power company park in her driveway and walk into her backyard. She goes out onto her patio and watches him spray-painting arrows on her grass. She calls to him, but he ignores her. So she walks out and joins him. He still refuses to talk to her. He thinks he doesn't have to answer her, even though he's on her property. He's just doing his job.

(2) A young couple is new in town and they want to obtain library cards. They stop at the library and ask questions at the front desk, but the librarian isn't good with people. She mumbles and doesn't smile, and whenever they ask questions she sighs and rolls her eyes. At several points in the conversation, there are awkward silences. The young couple manages to get their library cards, but it's an unpleasant experience.

(3) A professor grades his students severely and writes sarcastic comments on their papers. He frequently brings his students to tears by his caustic remarks in class. Nobody knows for sure what criteria he uses for grading. "It's a crap shoot," students say. But the professor has tenure and the department chairman will not listen to students' complaints.

(4) There's a nurse (or CT Scan specialist or Upper GI technician or... you fill in the blank) who barks orders at sick patients and makes them tremble in fear.

I could go on, but you get the idea. We've all met these kinds of people. They're in positions of service, but they don't see it that way. And because they don't, they're not only giving poor service; they're actually hurting others.

We can't do much about them (except pray for them and bless them, which may have positive results), but we can make sure that *we're* not part of the problem. That's what this book has been all about. We should examine ourselves prayerfully and make sure we're not perceived that way by others. There's a lot of poor treatment going on out there, and hopefully we're not perpetuating it.

But the tide is turning. More and more, employers expect their workers to become service-minded. Sometimes the secular culture wants the same thing Jesus wants, but for different reasons. This is one of those times. Because we're working within a service-driven economy, managers are increasingly aware that their employees must pay more attention to service issues. This is true even of back-office departments where there's no direct customer contact. The new motto is becoming something like this: "The people in other departments are our clients."

Some employees don't like the trend. A woman in operations once told me, "You people"—in other words, "you CSRs"—"you bend over backwards for the customer, but we don't do that over here." And why don't they? Because they don't have to. Since they're insulated from customer complaints, they don't feel obligated to help. And until recently, they believed they were morally superior to us CSRs because, unlike us, they didn't give in to clients' childish demands. But now their managers are pressuring them to be more responsive to others' needs, and they're starting to do it—begrudgingly.

The way they act reminds me of something that happened years ago when I worked in the darkroom of a printing company. The guys from the pressroom were sometimes in a hurry to get their plates from us, and one day a coworker of mine in the darkroom responded with humor. When the shop foreman nagged him for plates, my friend snarled: "Sure! Service with a smile!" He threw the work across the desk at the foreman and said, "Here's your service!" Then he bared his teeth, adding, "And here's your smile!"

My friend was joking, of course, but it illustrates the point. As more and more people in non-service jobs are expected to offer "customer service," they're doing it, but with thinly-veiled disgust.

For those who want to imitate Christ, however, this emphasis on service should be an encouraging trend, even if it means that their own job descriptions will change. As Christians, we're already in the business of serving and blessing others, no matter what we're actually paid to do.

Jesus asked, "[W]ho is greater, the one who is at the table or the one who serves? Is it not the one at the table? But I am among you as one who serves" (Luke 22:27). And that was the very reason for which he was born. "For the Son of Man came not to be served but to serve" (Matthew 20:28; Mark 10:45).

"A disciple is not above the teacher, nor a slave above the master; it is enough for the disciple to be *like* the teacher, and the slave *like* the master" (Matthew 10:24-25, emphasis added).

"You call me Teacher and Lord—and you are right, for that is what I am. So if I, your Lord and Teacher, have washed your feet, you also ought to wash one another's feet" (John 13:13-14).

We can call ourselves Christians, but if we don't bend over backwards for others then we haven't caught the vision of the One who came "not to be served but to serve." I've shared that vision with you in these pages. Christ wants to redeem the world through us. That's the secret of deep and abiding rest: to become increasingly better at letting *Christ* do the serving *through* us. And that's true for all of us, no matter what profession we're in.

If we're serious about imitating Christ then we shouldn't be satisfied thinking of ourselves as CSRs or computer programmers, attorneys or copy editors, realtors or police officers. We know that we're infinitely more than the individual roles we play in society. All together, we're the body of Christ. Through us—through *all* of us who profess him as Teacher, Savior, and Lord—Christ wants to bless and redeem the world. We must all do our part in every way we can, even on the job. Those of us who are CSRs are especially fortunate, for customer service work provides us with unique opportunities, as I have already shown throughout this book. Every call is a fresh chance for Christ to serve someone through us. And as we let that happen, the Kingdom of God advances.

Maybe that sounds grandiose, but that's the good news: that Christ knows and has redeemed each of us individually and is calling all of us collectively to be agents of change in this world by the power of the Holy Spirit. If we take that mandate seriously, it will affect everything we do. *Everything.* Even our jobs. Even the job of customer service.

## *Questions for Reflection and Discussion*

1. Are you tired? Can you identify the things you do that make you feel that way? Can you name the things that

energize you?

2. Do you believe that Christ can give you the deep and abiding rest you need? How can you claim that rest even in the middle of a busy work day?

3. Has it ever occurred to you that you are called to be part of the body of Christ even in your role as a CSR? Have you learned anything in this book that will help you fulfill that calling?

4. Are there any lingering questions or concerns that this study hasn't answered? Have you considered asking God about them?

# ABOUT THE AUTHOR

Ron Johnson has extensive experience working in customer service call centers, both as a frontline CSR and as a manager. After earning his PhD in Philosophy from Saint Louis University, he taught at colleges in St. Louis and Cincinnati. He currently teaches extension courses for Spring Arbor University and lives in Portage, Michigan, with his wife Nancy and daughter Emily. He leads workshops and seminars on finding points of contact with God in everyday life, particularly at work and at school. He blogs about these subjects at *Spiritual Adventures in the Workplace*. The site is: http://rjmythicadventures2.wordpress.com.

Made in the USA
Lexington, KY
18 March 2012